RACING
A Beginner's Manual

Fernhurst Books

www.fernhurstbooks.co.uk

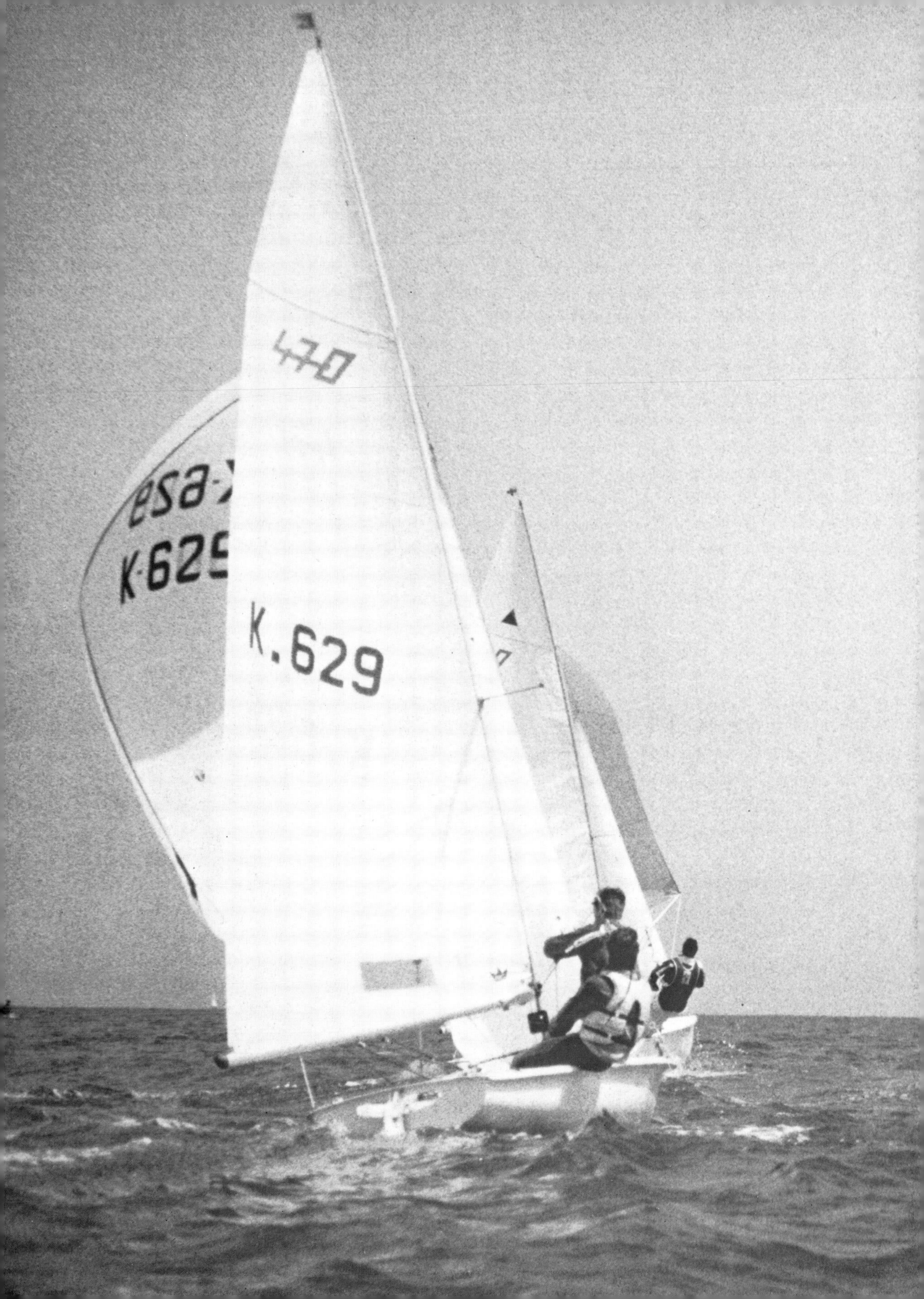
470
K.629

RACING
A Beginner's Manual

John Caig
&
Tim Davison

First published 1988 by Fernhurst Books, Duke's Path, High St, Arundel, BN18 9AJ, UK

ISBN 1 898660 88 3

Acknowledgements

The publishers would like to thank John Driscoll (National Sailing Coach), and Rob Andrews and John Derbyshire (RYA National Racing Coaches) for their comments on the manuscript; John Caig and Mike Curtis for loaning and crewing the boats used in the photographic sessions; and Walton Sailing Club for providing facilities for photography.

Photographs

All photographs by John Woodward with the exception of the following:
Julia Claxton: pages 2-3, 24, 51.
Tim Hore: pages 18-19, 21, 27 (both), 28 (left), 29 (top right), 32 (both), 33, 54 (bottom right), 57.
I.L.C.A: page 13.
Yachting Photographics: pages 6, 7, 20, 31, 40.
The photographs by John Woodward were printed by Julia Claxton.

Design by John Woodward
Artwork by Malcolm Walker
Cover design by Simon Balley
Composition by Book Economy Services, Burgess Hill

Printed in China through World Print

Contents

Introduction

This book is intended as a guide for people who have already learned to sail and would like to go a step further and start racing.

Many people catch the 'bug' after their first race, and it remains with them for the rest of their lives. Why is this? There are those who are naturally competitive and always want to test their skill against others. Some are less competitive but enjoy racing because it offers the best opportunity to get the best out of their boats. There is nothing like a few races to show you just how badly you are sailing!

You will probably be itching to enter a race before you have read to the end of this book, so we have laid out the first four chapters to give you enough knowledge to take part in a race with some degree of confidence. The remainder of the book is designed to help you improve your performance, and a glossary of terms used in racing is included at the end.

Many successful racing skippers start their racing careers by crewing with more experienced helms. It can be an advantage to get the feel for racing before you start out on your own, but it is by no means essential. You may learn faster by finding your own way, and this book will help you do just that.

We hope you enjoy your racing as much as we have done, and continue to do. It will give you an absorbing hobby for life. Good sailing!

John Caig and Tim Davison

1 Choosing a boat

If you don't already have a boat you may be wondering what to buy. If you have been crewing for someone then you will already know a little about what you might want. But if you are starting from scratch you have two choices: either join a club first (which limits your choice of boat) or buy a boat first (which limits your choice of club).

It's probably best to visit your nearest club and consider the suitability of the boats they sail. If you have a family and you intend to race with them you need a boat large enough to take them. If not, then one of the singlehanders may well be best for you. Also, take physical factors into account. If you are not particularly heavy then you will be wise to consider a boat with a small sail area which will not be too strenuous. For example, if you buy a Laser and you weigh only 120 lbs (54kg) you will begin to be at a disadvantage when the wind reaches 15 knots. In a 420 you could be in with the champs in any weather.

Another consideration is, of course, cost. You have to be able to buy your boat, but you also need to be aware of the cost of maintaining it, including buying new sails when it becomes necessary (at least every other season, if you want to stay competitive).

It's often advisable to go for a used boat at first, buying a new one when you have learned enough to know how you want it to be fitted out. Don't be afraid to buy and sell boats: why stick in a class you aren't enjoying or in a boat that's holding you back?

There's a huge variety of boats out there: one of them is sure to be right for you.

2　What is a race?

Most dinghy races are sailed round a number of marker buoys specified by the Sailing or Race Committee, and called 'The course'.

You have to round each buoy in a specified direction. 'Buoy X to port' for example means you round it anticlockwise, leaving it on the port side of your boat. Similarly, 'all marks to starboard' means you round them all clockwise. You will often see a shorthand form such as 1S 2P etc; this means leave buoy 1 to port, buoy 2 to starboard, and so on. Sometimes the buoys are shown on a coloured background, red indicating a buoy to be left to port, green meaning leave it to starboard.

The course

This is always laid down in the sailing instructions, which are posted on a notice board or handed out as a printed sheet.

Sailing instructions are always given in writing and the rules prevent their being given orally. It is important that competitors study these instructions before the race.

There are several types of course depending

Below left: Rounding a mark to port.
Below right: Rounding a mark to starboard.

on the local geography, but most are triangular in shape and are intended to test all points of sailing. The start is across an imaginary line between two points (often a committee boat and buoy) and is usually signalled by the lowering of a flag and the sounding of a horn or gun.

All boats must be behind this line when the starting signal is made. A warning signal (usually ten minutes before the start) and preparatory signal (with five minute to go) allow competitors to start their watches and do their own countdown.

If there is any discrepancy, the time is taken from the preparatory signal.

Sometimes a distance mark is laid to keep competitors clear of the committee boat: you are not allowed to sail between them. Note that this mark is not necessarily *on* the startline, in fact it is usually over the line.

The first leg is usually upwind to the first mark, and most boats will make a number of tacks to reach it. This should have the effect of spreading out the fleet so there is not too much congestion at the first mark.

Subsequent legs are 'off the wind', and made up of reaches or runs, eventually ending back near the starting area. The course is often repeated, the number of rounds being specified in the sailing instructions.

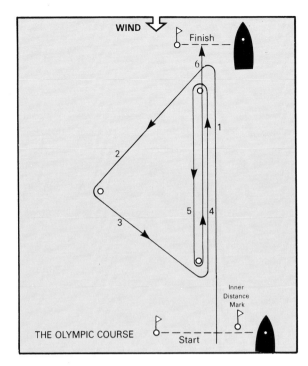

THE OLYMPIC COURSE

If the wind drops the race can be shortened by a shortened course signal which is usually code flag S – a blue rectangle on a white background. The race then ends at the next mark after the signal was made. Finishes are usually into the wind and entail crossing a finishing line between two marks or a committee boat and mark.

Below: The startline lies between the committee boat mast and the outer distance mark. The inner distance mark keeps the competitors clear of the committee boat; you must not pass between the two, so this Fireball will be disqualified!

The Olympic course
The Olympic course is so named because it is used in Olympic competition. It aims to offer the fairest race, with all points of sailing included. The start is upwind for the reasons already mentioned. The second and third legs are reaches; sometimes one is a close reach and the other a broad reach. At the leeward mark the course turns upwind once more. A run follows the second rounding of the weather mark. This sequence of legs is repeated until the finish, which is either between the weather mark and a committee boat or at a finish line upwind of the weather mark.

Where space does not permit such a course – for instance on a small inland reservoir – then the course should be set to give the best balance of beating, reaching and running.

Handicap racing

When boats of different types are going to race together a handicap race is organised. There are two main ways of doing this.

Conventional handicap races
All boats start on the same signal, as in a one-design race, but their finishing times are recorded by the Race Officer. When all the boats have finished, their times are multiplied by a handicap correction figure to provide the final race results. This correction is arrived at by considering the results of many club races over many years. It cannot be completely fair, particularly in the case of boats that perform very differently in differing conditions (such as catamarans), but nevertheless it can be a basis for quite satisfactory inter-class racing.

Pursuit races
Here the starting time of each boat is determined by its handicap number. The slowest set off first, and the race is run for a predetermined length of time. The finish line is not laid until the finish time is due, and the first across the line wins. In order to make the final results as fair as possible for slower boats who are trailing, a number of finish lines could be laid simultaneously. In fact the fairest results would be determined by an aerial photograph – not all that practical for your average club race!

3 Basic racing rules

You may feel that you need to know all the rules before you take part in your first race, but if you waited until you knew them all you would never get started – there are quite a number and some need a lot of experience to interpret.

A few basic rules are all you need to begin with and many a club sailor never gets around to learning more (although of course they are always intending to!) When you want to know more read *The Rules in Practice* by Bryan Willis also published by Fernhurst Books.

The need for racing rules

No sport or game can be successful without rules of some sort, and yacht racing is no exception. What's more, unlike football and cricket there are no referees or umpires, so observance of the rules relies on the obedience and honesty of the competitors. When there is a disagreement the only option is a *protest* which is heard by an independent body of knowledgeable yachtsmen called a Protest Committee. The word protest is often misunderstood by non-sailing people, but those involved with the sport soon come to realise that it is the only fair method of sorting out who is in the right in a particular rules incident. The International Yacht Racing Union (IYRU) Rules are used throughout the world in local, international and Olympic competition. While some variations can be made to suit local club conditions the basic rules remain the same wherever you race. So what are they?

1 Port gives way to starboard

You are on starboard tack when the boom is on the port side and the wind is coming from your starboard side. A boat sailing on starboard tack has the right of way and, unless there is danger of a collision, must hold a steady course when a port tack boat is near (so as not to mislead her). Most boats will start the race on starboard tack because it is important to have right of way in

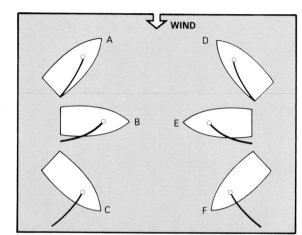

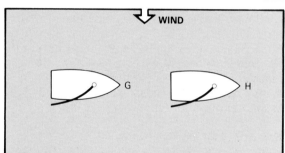

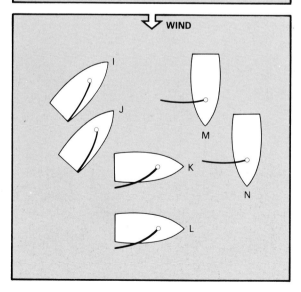

the congested area of the start line. In the diagram D, E and F have right of way over A, B and C who have to keep clear.

2 The overtaking boat must keep clear

When you are approaching another boat from behind you must be sure that you keep clear. In the diagram G is overtaking and is not allowed to sail into the back of H. This situation is very likely to occur at the start when the boats nearest to the start line slow up and those just behind tend to run them down.

3 A windward boat shall keep clear of a leeward boat

The windward boat is the one that is nearer to the wind than the other – that is, it is upwind of the other. The rule says that it has to keep clear of the downwind boat. This rule is one of natural justice. Since a boat being overtaken to windward will have its wind taken away, it is only fair that it should be given the right to defend its position. The leeward boat (the one furthest from the wind) may turn up towards the wind (or *luff*) and the windward boat has to keep clear.

This rule is of particular importance at the start when the boats are close together, and on the reach when everyone is fighting for clear wind. In the diagram I must keep clear of J, K must keep clear of L and N must keep clear of M.

Below: 122417 on port gives way to 72469 on starboard – but 72469 must keep to her course.

Above: The windward boat (right) must keep clear.
Below: The overtaking boat (left) must keep clear.

4 A boat must give room at a mark to another boat overlapping it on the inside

This means that as two or more boats are about to round a mark the one on the outside must give room to the one on the inside – if the inside boat can establish an overlap, in proper time, on the boat outside her. Proper time is judged by drawing an imaginary circle around the buoy with a radius of two boat lengths. The inside boat needs to establish its overlap before the outside one enters this circle. The inside crew often shout 'Water!' to establish their rights, though this is not essential according to the rules. In the diagram, O has the right to round inside P.

5 Touching a mark

If you touch a mark, sail well clear. Immediately make one complete turn (360), keeping clear of all other boats. Then sail on.

Alternative penalties

Occasionally you may infringe a racing rule, particularly when you are new to racing. In the past, if you infringed a rule (or touched a mark) you were expected to retire immediately, or make a protest if you considered you were in the right. Today the sailing instructions *may* allow you to carry out an alternative penalty.

The most usual alternative penalty is the 720-degree turn. When a boat is in collision with another and the skipper considers that he is in the wrong, he may make two complete circles (beginning in either direction) as soon as he can get clear after the incident, and thus avoid having to retire from the race.

Protests

You should bear in mind that every time a collision occurs between two boats, one or both will have infringed a rule. If you consider that you are in the right and the other competitor does not do a 720 degree turn, you should inform him that you are going to protest by hailing 'Protest'. (If your boat is more than six metres long you also have to display a red flag with a swallowtail cut out of it.) After the race fill out a protest form. It is best to seek advice from someone experienced who can make sure that you quote

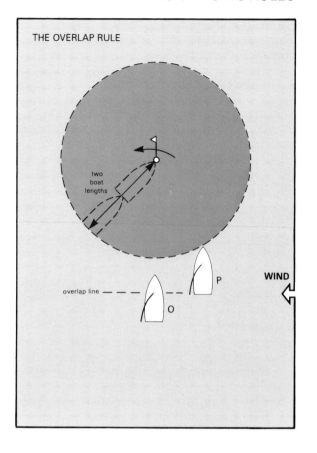

THE OVERLAP RULE

two boat lengths

overlap line

P

O

WIND

the appropriate rule and indeed check that you are probably in the right!

Remember is it not unsporting to protest. Since there is no referee watching your race the rules need to be implemented afterwards. Without protests anarchy would reign!

Armed with at least an understanding of the rules above, you are ready to take part in your first race.

Golden rules

★ Port gives way to starboard.

★ The overtaking boat keeps clear.

★ The windward boat keeps clear of the leeward boat.

★ At a mark, the outside boat gives room to the inside boat (provided the overlap was established in proper time).

4   Your first race

Don't forget that, beginner or not, you will be a very welcome addition to the fleet. Those who usually do well, the 'hot shots', will be only too pleased to come home having beaten a larger fleet. Those nearer the back of the fleet will welcome the chance to perhaps beat someone! Don't be disappointed if you are last – just give it a go! Do remember that, particularly in the heat of the start, some competitors can get a bit excited and may shout at you if they think you are infringing the rules. Don't let this worry you; they may not have had time to realise you were a beginner and you'll probably find that back in the clubhouse they are quite decent. But do speak to them about any such incident afterwards, particularly if you are unsure of which rule you may have infringed. It's a good chance to learn as well as make friends.

Now, how should you approach the race? First you must read the sailing instructions or at very least speak to a friend and establish the essential information (it's not a good idea to expect to follow everyone else). The course referred to in this chapter will be a triangular one with the sequence beat-reach-reach-beat-run-beat, known as the Olympic course. In practice you are likely to encounter more complicated courses at your local club. Nevertheless, the Olympic course described covers all the relevant points of sailing. (A diagram of the Olympic course is given in Chapter 2.)

To begin with you need to know the startline. This will be an imaginary line between two points and often limited in length by extra marker buoys. Typically the startline is defined as a line between the mast on a committee boat and a buoy, with a limit mark near the committee boat. This inner distance limit mark is not necessarily on the line, but boats must not pass between it and the committee boat. The committee boat may be replaced by an onshore mast or pole which may be portable or permanent.

Next you need to know the course: the order in which the buoys are to be rounded and on which side. If a mark is to be left to port then you are required to pass around it on its right-hand side (anticlockwise) leaving the buoy on your left. If you have any doubt where to go, make yourself a course card, put it in a clear plastic bag and tape it to the boat.

You also need to know the number of laps to be sailed and where the finish is. During the race you must watch the committee boat: if code flag S is flown it means the course is being shortened because the wind is falling light.

Finally you must know the time of the start. Do try to get on the water in plenty of time: this is the most common failing of beginner and expert alike. Time always seems to go faster than you expect and arriving at the start without sorting out your strategy can be a costly mistake.

The start

You can expect the start to be upwind (to windward), so plan to start on starboard tack about one third of the way down the line from the starboard end. (Later we will discuss how to choose the favoured end but, for the moment, assuming a line of 200 ft (60 m) or less, the first-timer should do as suggested.)

Try a few practice runs, timing yourself to get an idea how far you travel in, say, 60 seconds. If the wind is light try to keep close to the line in case it drops further, leaving you stranded. This is of particular importance if there is any current taking you away from the line.

Watch out for the warning signal. This will be a sound signal accompanied by your class flag and is usually five minutes before the start. Start your stopwatch on this signal and check it at the preparatory signal four minutes before the start. Remember that the racing rules come into force after this second signal so keep a good look out (as you should at all times).

From your previous trial runs you will have established how far you can expect to travel in one minute. Try to be somewhere near this one-minute distance from the line at about one and a half minutes before the start. This will allow you to slow your approach as you get closer to the line. The easiest way to slow up is to ease the sails until they are half flapping, sheeting them in again when more speed is needed. Heading closer to the wind without sheeting in will also slow you up. Be careful not to drop down on other boats to leeward or

you may be greeted by shouts of 'Up up!' indicating that you must luff to avoid a collision. Try to approach the line with space below you, so you can free off (ease sails and steer away from the wind) at the last minute and cross the line with maximum speed. In any event if the helmsman keeps an eye on the boat to leeward it will help him judge his own start. In the meantime the crew should look to weather and warn the helmsman if the weather boat is about to sail over the top of them. You will hear a further sound signal one minute before the start, and a signal at the start - that makes four signals in all.

The first beat

Once the gun has gone and you have crossed the line you will be beating towards the first mark. Don't be discouraged by the fact that the

Left: 122417 is tacking too close, and the starboard Laser has to take avoiding action. Above: Here 122417 has opted to pass astern of the starboard-tack boat rather than risk infringing the rule (and losing a friend. . . .)

boats around you are going faster or closer to the wind. Most novices tend not to pull the mainsail in close enough. As you gain experience you will find that sail trim is quite critical in getting the best speed out of your boat. The important thing at this stage is to keep steering closer to the wind until the sails begin to flap (luff) and the boat begins to slow, and then bearing away until full speed is achieved once more. The ability to spot the moment just before the boat begins to slow is important in your development of good upwind speed. You will soon learn to continually luff and bear away *subtly* so you can respond to the continuous changes in the wind's direction. Don't follow boats that are only half a dozen boat lengths ahead of you; they will slow you up because they interfere with your wind. Tack away to get

clear air. On the other hand don't go way off on your own; there is probably a very good reason why the majority of the racing fleet is going the other way.

From time to time you may encounter other boats on the opposite tack. If you are on starboard you have the right of way and *must* hold your course. Call 'Starboard' if you think the crew of the other boat haven't seen you. Even on starboard you should keep a good look-out. In the event of substantial damage you will still carry some responsibility for not keeping clear even though you had the right of way! If you are on port tack you must keep clear of a boat on starboard either by tacking or bearing away under her stern. If you are not confident of staying ahead after a tack you would do best to pass under her stern. (If you tack and she then sails over you you will be slowed unnecessarily.)

Below, left to right: This perfectly-timed tack by 122417 (on port) enables her to put a lee-bow on 72469, giving her a tactical advantage (see page 35 for lee-bowing).

Remember that when you need to bear away to duck someone's stern you must ease the mainsheet. If you don't, the weather helm will make bearing off much more difficult, particularly if it is windy, and you risk a collision. Ease sails as you bear away and trim them in again quickly as you luff up: this way you will lose very little distance – in fact you will momentarily be able to point higher just after crossing behind another boat, due to her effect on the wind direction.

Try to approach the windward mark on starboard tack if other boats are likely to arrive at the same time: a port tack approach is risky.

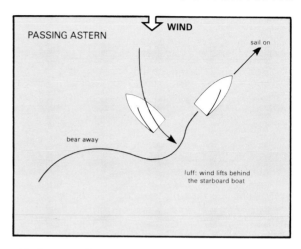

The reach

Once around the windward mark you will be on a reach. Ease out the sheets until the sails are just about to flap. Pull the centreboard up to about halfway and head directly towards the next mark unless there is a very good reason to do otherwise. Concentrate on maximum speed by careful trimming of the sails. If you begin to overtake another boat you must be prepared for her to suddenly luff you – that is, steer rapidly up into the wind to stop you overtaking. To avoid

Below: When rounding the weather mark, let the mainsheet out progressively (left). If you keep it pinned in the boat will heel violently to leeward (centre); let it out too fast and you dunk the crew (right).

this keep well clear of boats to leeward. If there is a collision you will be in the wrong.

If another boat does luff you away from the direct course, it's probably best to ease your sheets, slow up, and bear off under her stern.

The next buoy is the gybe mark. Should you be overlapped on the inside you must give plenty of room for that boat to round inside you. Gybe firmly with the centreboard half up, and make sure that at the moment the boom comes across you straighten up to prevent the boat spinning up into the wind. Once on the new reach, head straight for the next mark: you will lose out if you sail a curved path to windward of the rhumb line.

Rounding the leeward mark differs from the previous one in that you will need the centreboard right down just before going round.

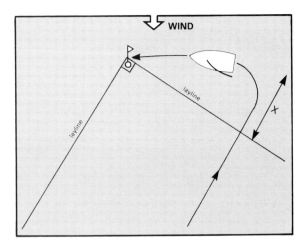

Steer a little wide as you approach it, sheeting in the sails as you tighten up round the mark.

Now you are on the beat once more. This time the boats will be spaced out a little and you will probably be further behind. Don't worry, just concentrate on sailing as fast as possible.

Without following close behind anyone in particular, follow the general direction of the leaders; they are probably doing the right thing. Try not to overstand the windward mark – if you go past the layline (see diagram) you will need to reach down to the buoy, wasting valuable distance (X on the diagram).

The run

After rounding the windward mark for the second time, the next leg is a run downwind to the leeward mark. Raise the centreboard approximately three-quarters of the way up, and ease the sheets out all the way. The direct line to the leeward mark will usually be quickest, unless you are flying a spinnaker (or sailing a catamaran).

If it is at all windy, however, you must be careful not to gybe accidentally. The best way to avoid this is to sail a little higher than the dead run (when the wind is directly behind), gybing back towards the leeward mark when you reckon the new course will be another broad reach. If you are ahead of any boats keep an eye on them: don't let them creep up on you and take your wind. If they do, either luff up or steer off to leeward to keep your wind clear. Try to approach the mark on the gybe that you will be rounding on; having to gybe *at* the mark is best

avoided. Don't forget to lower the board before rounding!

The final beat will probably be similar to the previous one. Keep trying to improve your speed and assessing how fast you are going in relation to the others. Experiment with sheet tension and the angle that you sail to the wind until you feel you are getting the best speed.

The finish

Make sure that this really is the finish by watching the leaders to be sure that they are stopping. Sail all the way through the finish line: in many clubs the rules prevent you recrossing the line, so be sure to sail around one of the ends on your way home. Now all you have to do is sign the declaration form, if the rules require it, to say that you completed the course without infringing any of the rules.

What did you think of it?

By now you will know whether racing is for you. In all probability you will be hooked for life. Perhaps you may be tempted to think there isn't much to it and that after a few races you'll know it all. However, you will very soon come to realise that there is an infinite amount you still have to learn – and therein lies the true challenge of dinghy racing. The rest of this book should at least serve to open your eyes!

Golden rules

★ Read the sailing instructions.

★ Don't get too far from the startline.

★ Start on starboard tack.

★ Keep clear of boats to leeward at the start.

★ Try not to sail in dirty wind.

★ Approach the windward mark on starboard tack.

★ Steer a straight course on each reach.

★ Keep going to the finish.

5 Helming and crewing skills

The more you sail your boat the faster you will be able to sail it.

It's a very good idea to go out and practise, but once you start racing you may well find that practice becomes boring. The advantage of practising over racing is that you can devote more time to thinking about the way you are doing things, and repeat individual manoeuvres until you are happy with them. But when you're racing you are too concerned about losing even one place to risk a new technique. So try to organise some practice.

To begin with, practise in medium winds. If you sail a two-man boat and are lucky enough to have a regular crew, now is the time to work up some teamwork. Remember your crew is not a mind-reader. Only when you have practised and raced together a great deal will you be able to do things without a word. Explain what you intend to do *before* you do it so that you can both be ready to perform in unison.

At first, practise by sailing around two marks lined up with the wind, doing lots of tacks on the beats and plenty of gybes on the runs. Work on your technique, and try to make it fast and fluent.

Tacking

In most dinghies it pays to roll tack the boat in anything but the heaviest of winds. This is achieved by co-ordinating the heel of the boat and its angle to the wind throughout the tack.

- Heel the boat a little more than normal.

- As you begin to push the tiller away, both of you should hike out hard on the weather side.

- Only cross to the other side after the boat has passed through the eye of the wind.

- If you have a jib hold it aback until the boat is past head to wind; this helps spin the boat round.

- Pull the boat up sharply to the normal sailing angle.

A well-executed roll tack should mean very little loss of speed. In boats with very round sections you can actually speed up when roll tacking excessively. Since it is not legal to come out of a tack faster than you go into it, you may have to subdue your roll tacks! In most boats

Prepare to tack . . .

Push the tiller away . . .

Roll the boat . . .

and with most beginners this will definitely not be a problem. Quite obviously, the longer the boat stays head to wind with the sails flapping the more she will slow down, so try to tack quickly.

Always try to tack when the boat is going fast, so you maintain sufficient momentum through the turn. Avoid two tacks in quick succession unless they are absolutely essential. Also remember that when sailing in waves you should try to tack on the crest of the wave, when the bow and stern are less deep in the water, rather than in a trough. Experience will help you tack through the correct angle automatically, without ending up too far off the wind or pointing too close to it.

Gybing

You won't gybe as many times in a race as you tack, but a bad gybe in heavy weather can end in a capsize and many lost places. Begin by practising in medium conditions and always remember that you should make the boat gybe when *you* want and not when *it* decides to. In this way you and your crew can be ready to move your weight and steer the boat round at exactly the right moment.

To achieve a smooth gybe it is important that the boat rolls towards the side where you are sitting (the weather side) just before the boom comes across. If the boat is heeling away from you the weather helm that this causes will make

bearing off extremely difficult. Assuming that you are not flying a spinnaker, the sequence of events as you turn around the gybe mark should be as follows:

- Take the mainsheet straight from the boom to get a direct pull.

- Bear away as you draw level with the mark, and at the same time lean out.

- Watch the leech of the mainsail. When it lifts you know the boom is ready to come across. Continue bearing away, giving the mainsheet a pull and calling your crew to help the boom across.

- As the boom comes over move quickly to the other side. At the same time reverse the helm to stop the boat continuing round towards the wind and broaching.

- At the same time your crew should also move quickly to the weather side. Unhampered by thoughts of steering he should be able to use his weight to counter the new heeling moment of the mainsail, while sheeting the jib to help reduce weather helm.

If the wind is gusting you will find, rather surprisingly, that it is much easier to gybe when you are going fast. This is because the pressure of wind on the sails is lightest when the boat is moving quickly away from the wind. This lets the boom come over much easier. Confidence is the hallmark of gybing in a blow!

Centre the tiller . . .   *Hike out hard . . .*   *And sail off .*

Beating

You must learn to sail to windward by second nature. There are many decisions to be taken during a beat: has the wind shifted; should we tack; which way is paying off; where are the competition heading? While you're thinking about that lot you're sailing the boat through the water on automatic pilot.

You will discover that as you pinch (sail too close to the wind) a number of things happen: the sails begin to lift near the luff (leading edge), the boat starts to heel towards you, and you will actually hear the boat slowing up as the wave sound against the hull diminishes. Even with your eyes closed you should be aware that you are pinching. Bearing too far off the wind is rather less obvious, so the art of beating is to sail closer to the wind until you get the 'messages' that tell you to bear off.

Apart from accurate steering you will need to pay attention to sail trim. The main and jib need to be pulled in fairly tightly so the boat can point quite close to the wind. Generally, pull in the mainsheet until the top telltale on the leech (the one by the top batten) breaks. The tighter you pull down on the mainsheet the more the mast will bend, flattening the sail. Also, the tension down the leech will reduce its twist. The conditions (wind strength and waves) will dictate the correct sail shape for beating.

- A flat sail is required for strong winds because a deeply-cambered sail will produce too great a side force (and heeling moment) as well as increased drag.

- Medium winds require a fuller sail.

- Very light winds once again need a fairly flat sail so that the wind can flow across it without turbulence. Achieve this by inducing mast bend without much sheet tension so that a degree of twist remains in the sail. This is best done by removing chocks at deck level, raking the spreaders aft or prebending under rig tension (see Tuning).

Jib sheeting is also important. Too tight and the sail will be too flat, too loose and the leech

curls which reduces power and stops the boat pointing. Generally, ease the jibsheet in lighter winds, moving the fairlead forward to prevent too much twisting off at the top. Sheet harder in medium winds, with the fairlead central. Move the fairlead aft in strong winds and play the jibsheet to keep the boat on her feet – that is, let the sheet out a bit in gusts.

It is a good idea to attach telltales to the luff of your jib. These are short wool streamers about 3 in (8 cm) long fixed at intervals on each side of the jib about 4 in (10 cm) behind the luff. Telltales act as guides for steering and also for sheeting angle. When you are sailing closehauled at the optimum angle to the wind the telltales should stream back horizontally on both sides of the jib. As you luff closer to the wind the telltales on the weather side will fly upwards. If the upper telltale breaks first then the sail is too twisted and the fairlead may need moving forward. But if the lower one breaks first the jib sheet is too tight or the fairlead needs to come aft to induce more twist.

Many helmsmen use the telltales all the time as a guide to good windward sailing; for others general 'feel and heel' are a more precise guide. But if you see the leeward telltales break you are definitely too far off the wind.

Beating in light winds

Because side forces are no problem in light winds, use full sails to increase drive. (In very light winds full sails don't work because the airstream is too weak to follow a large curve.)

Pointing close to the wind is no longer important: keeping the boat moving is the top priority. Choose tacks that will take you towards increased wind, as indicated by wavelets on the water. Move around the boat slowly, if you need to move at all, because violent movements will shake the wind out of the sails. Disregard the normal need to keep the boat flat, allowing her to heel about 5-10 degrees. This is advantageous in two ways. Firstly it helps keep the sails full by gravity alone. Secondly the wetted surface area on most dinghies is reduced. Sitting forward in the boat also reduces wetted area. Smooth roll tacks are essential in these conditions.

Left: You should be thinking about tactics and strategy on the beat, not how to sail the boat. Right: Keep the boat upright in medium to strong winds – you'll go faster that way.

Beating in strong winds

As the wind strength increases beyond the point where you can hold the boat flat by hiking hard, you will need to lose power to prevent excessive heeling. If you let the boat heel you will need to pull hard on the tiller to counter the increased weather helm, which causes drag and slows the boat. Also, since the hull is designed to travel through the water upright, resistance increases as she heels. Keep the boat dead upright. Let the jibsheet out a little.

Flatten the main by:

1 Pulling hard (very hard) on the vang (kicking strap).

2 Removing chocks from in front of the mast at deck level (this lets the mast bend).

It is also a good idea to rake the mast further aft than normal; this reduces the overlap between the jib and main and reduces power. Now all you have to do is sail the boat to windward, keeping her flat by playing the mainsheet in and out. If a gust hits you, let out

an arm's length of mainsheet and bear away a little to pick up speed. Once the boat is motoring, pull in the sheet again.

In boats such as the Laser, that rely on an extremely bent mast to maintain a sensible sail shape, easing the mainsheet lets the mast straighten which results in a fuller sail (despite a tight vang, which will always stretch). In these boats an alternative method of depowering is preferable, such as feathering.

Feathering is a technique of 'pinching' very close to the wind, causing the front edge of the sail to lift, then bearing off before the boat slows too much. Successive luffs have the advantage of ensuring you are sailing close to the wind as well as helping to keep the boat upright. It is a technique that needs to be practised, and it is only effective in smooth water.

In waves the beginner is advised to ease the sheet a good deal and sail well off the wind. Remember to sit close to your crew (if you have one) to reduce pitching (bow and stern going up and down); indeed any weight in the bow or stern is detrimental in waves.

Steering in waves is an art; keep the tiller and mainsheet in constant motion, luffing up (and pulling in the sheet) as the boat goes up each wave and bearing away (and letting out the sheet) as the bow reaches each crest. Pick up speed down the back of the wave before luffing up for the next.

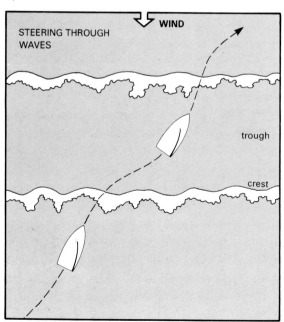

Reaching

Many feel that after a long hard beat the reach is the time to relax. I'm sorry to tell you that the reverse is true: if you work hard you can gain many places on the reach, particularly in planing conditions and in big fleets.

Good reaching speed relies on careful sail trim and on keeping the boat flat.

Ease both main and jib until they lift on the luff, then sheet in a little. Keep trying this sequence to ensure that you haven't missed a windshift.

You need only moderate vang (kicking strap) tension to stop the boom lifting and the upper sail being freed off too much.

In the absence of other considerations, such as wind changes or other boats, try to sail the direct rhumb line between the marks. A curved course can add many boat lengths of distance. Be careful not to steer too high a course: if you line up the bow with the mark you will automatically sail too high (see photo). Make an allowance for this by 'pointing' well below the mark.

As a gust arrives ease sheets and bear off a little. This helps in three ways:

- In the increased wind of a gust your speed does not decrease much as you bear away. Later, in the inevitable lull, you can *increase* speed by luffing back towards the rhumb line.

- You offset the immediate heeling force.

- Most important, you carry the gust longer as you sail down with it.

As this gust passes, pull in the sheets and luff back up to increase your speed and to take you to windward so you reach the next gust sooner.

Always keep the boat flat so that its planing surface is horizontal. Sit out hard, bearing off at the same time if the boat begins to heel. Only in very light weather is a little heel permissible to reduce wetted area and keep the sails full.

The centreboard should be about half up. This reduces wetted area and also reduces weather helm, while still countering the sideforces.

Reaching in waves
You will need to move aft a little to keep the bow above the waves. Take the mainsheet straight from the boom. As you reach the top of a wave bear away, sheet in and try to plane down it.

Above: This Fireball is reaching straight for the buoy, although the sightline through the forestay suggests otherwise.

Sheeting in is essential to take account of the apparent wind which comes forward as you accelerate. These are probably the most exciting conditions you can race in, and practice will bring its rewards.

Running in light winds

Because the sail plan of most boats is unbalanced when running it is usually a good idea to heel the boat 5–10 degrees to weather to get the centre of effort of the sail over the centreline of the boat. (Boats with spinnakers are better balanced.) As a result less rudder is needed to keep the boat running straight (every time you use the rudder on a reach or a run the brakes go on). With most dinghies this weather heel will also reduce wetted area.

On a run it helps for the helmsman and crew to sit out on opposite sides. Their moment of inertia helps to prevent any roll starting. (In non-technical terms, the wind has to raise one of the crew if it wants to heel the boat.)

Running in strong winds

Though rather less exciting than the reach, a heavy weather run can be very demanding indeed. Your boat may become rather unstable

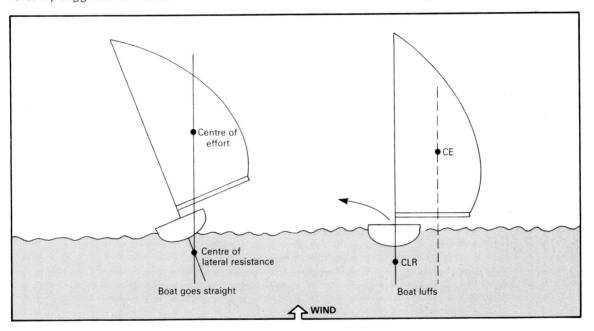

and develop a pronounced roll, while in a seaway she may try to nosedive.

You can greatly reduce these problems by steering firmly, sheeting correctly and moving your weight aft. Don't allow the mainsail out too far! If you do, any twist in the sail will allow the head to swing forward of the mast, producing a force to weather which makes you roll. So if you find yourself rolling to weather, pull in the mainsheet. If you heel to leeward let out the mainsheet. Don't raise the board too high – its depth in the water has a distinct damping effect.

Don't sit too far forward if you think the boat may nosedive. Sheeting in a little also helps by reducing forces at the top of the mast.

Rounding marks

Like all other 'set pieces', mark rounding needs practice. The objective is always to approach the mark wide, then turn slowly and smoothly round it, exiting very close to the buoy. In this way you avoid losing too much speed round the turn, and start the next leg in a good tactical position, free to carry on or tack.

Above, right to left: When you round a mark, come in wide and exit close.

Starting

A crowded startline is no place to find you're weak at slowing, stopping, flapping or accelerating. Practise on your own, well before the race, using a buoy. Reach up to it, then point into the wind and slow down. Try to 'hang' with your bow just off the buoy for two minutes at least. If you find you're going forwards, push out the boom. If you're drifting back, pull in the jib. If you're stuck in irons (head to wind) jerk the tiller towards you several times, or push out the boom.

Below: Practise sailing up to the line as slowly as possible, with your sails flapping.

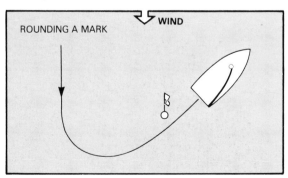

ROUNDING A MARK   WIND

Above: If you get stuck head to wind, back the jib to make the boat bear away.

Above: When it's time to go, pulling in the jib gives you instant acceleration.

Try sailing backwards in case you need to reverse over the startline – go head to wind, push out the boom and hold it against the shrouds. Then steer backwards (point the tiller the way you want the bow to swing).

Now practice accelerating off the line. Turn the

Below: Push out the boom to stop.

boat onto a close reach, gradually squeeze in the sails and luff slowly to close-hauled. Jerk the boat level, and you're away. The whole process should take about ten seconds.

Finally, set up a 33-foot (ten-metre) startline between two buoys, and practise starting through it giving yourself a two-minute and a one-minute 'gun'.

Golden rules

★ Practice makes perfect.

★ Keep the boat flat.

★ On a beat, sheet the main so that the top telltale just breaks.

★ Play the jibsheet – a couple of inches makes all the difference.

★ Sit forward in light winds.

★ You need flat sails when beating in very light and in strong winds.

★ You need full sails offwind.

★ On a reach luff in the lulls and bear away in the gusts.

★ Heel the boat to windward on a run.

★ To round a mark, approach it wide and leave it close.

★ Practise strategy: a crowded startline is no place to learn!

6   Boat preparation and equipment

You will by now have discovered that not everything on your boat works one hundred per cent. Little niggling things that you are prepared to put up with when cruising become major problems when you're in a race: jamb cleats that don't, rudders that unexpectedly come up half way down the reach, and mainsheets that don't run smoothly.

Once you become at all serious about racing you must also take boat preparation seriously. After each race you need to make a list of all the problems, then find the time to rectify them before you race again. Even if you haven't the time to attend to the problems immediately keep a running list of all items requiring attention, then have a blitz. The odd windless day spent sorting the boat can in itself be very satisfying.

But even before you sort out the gear, make sure the hull and foils are not letting you down.

Hull preparation

While the wind acting on the sails provides the force to move your boat forward, the friction of the water on the hull retards it. If you can reduce the friction to a minimum you will attain the best possible speed in any given conditions.

Turn your boat upside down and inspect the underwater surfaces. You should do this frequently anyway. Out of sight, out of mind is not a good policy: you may have damaged the hull without knowing it.

Apart from maintaining a smooth finish to the bottom it is very important on wooden boats to make certain that no bare wood has become exposed. Most modern wooden boats are epoxy coated. Once scratched, water may soak in causing both serious deterioration of the hull and an increase in weight. GRP soaks up water too, so any damage to the gel-coat needs immediate attention.

On the question of hull weight, you should at least be aware of how heavy your boat is. Nothing more sophisticated than two sets of bathroom scales – one supporting each end, their readings added together – are needed to get a good idea of the true weight. A hull weight of more than five per cent above the minimum allowed should be a cause for concern. Less than this is probably acceptable unless the boat is new or you are likely to be discouraged by knowing that your boat is overweight.

Any rough edges should be smoothed off with a rough file or sandpaper. Use fine wet-and-dry sandpaper even after the final coat of paint is applied if you are really keen!

In most classes slot gaskets are allowed to reduce the drag caused by water entering and leaving the centreboard case. If yours are made of rubber or mylar they may need replacing. Heavy sailcloth lasts longer.

Below: A well-designed centreboard slot, showing the pad of rubber at the forward end (left) and the slot aft to let the water drain out (right).

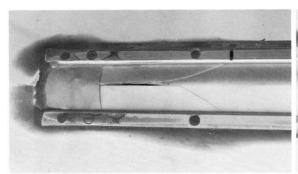
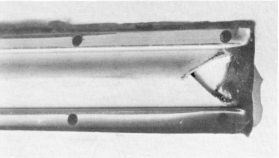

The foils

A smooth finish to the centreboard and rudder is even more important than the hull finish. Most of the hull moves through turbulent water, but the foils move through relatively smooth water and the percentage effect on speed reduction is much greater. Plastic Padding or a similar filler offers a quick solution to the chips that inevitably occur.

When you are smoothing off the foils, make sure that the front edge is well rounded, and the trailing edge is sharp (or slightly square). But do check that your class rules allow you to do all this.

Mast and rigging

If you have bought a new boat you should have chosen a mast whose section is most commonly used by the fleet leaders (in many one-design classes you will have no choice anyway).

Now you need to set the mast up. Provided it has shrouds, you have control over the rake of the mast (angle) and the tension of the rig. Note that the shroud lengths control the rake, while the jib halyard tension controls the rig tension (the tension in the jib luff *and* shrouds). If the mast has spreaders, then their length and angle may be adjusted to control the bend in the mast.

Below: Measure spreader deflection from the mast to a straight-edge laid between the tips.

The beginner should try and copy the precise set-up of one of the more successful boats; indeed you should be able to find someone who will be pleased to set up your boat for you. After all, if they are quite good they will not expect you, a beginner, to start beating them, and they have little to lose by helping you. So rule one is: seek advice on mast set-up.

But if help is unforthcoming, here is a rough do-it-yourself guide.

Rig tension

The first thing to do is set up the rig fairly tight by pulling on the jib halyard. You cannot assess the mast rake or bend until the tension is on. (Note that you set up the boat with the jib up but the mainsail down.) It is very important to be aware that the forestay on a dinghy is simply there to stop the mast falling down when the jib is removed. (If the class rules permit you might consider dispensing with the forestay altogether, using the halyard to hold up the mast after you take the jib down.)

It is of vital importance that the jib luff is tighter than the forestay. If this is not so the jib will sag, and this will introduce excessive fullness (camber) into the sail. This adversely affects how close to the wind you can point on the beat. (To overcome the distraction of a loose forestay waving around, a short piece of shock cord is often used to keep it artificially 'tight'.)

Below: The forestay must be looser than the jib luff. Use elastic to stop it flapping around.

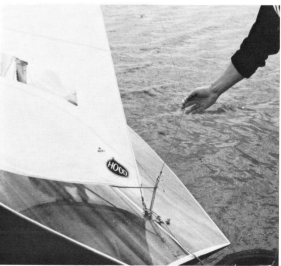

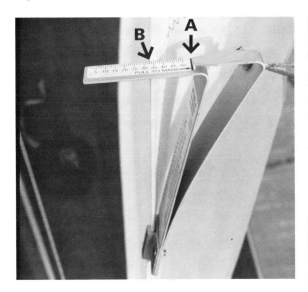

Above: To use a rig tension meter, hook it on the luff wire, pull it so the pointer reaches mark A, and read off the value by the wire (B).

Rig tension is controlled by the precise setting of the jib halyard – tensions of between 200 –350 lbs (90–160 kg) being typical. Read Lawrie Smith's *Tuning your Dinghy* for an in-depth treatment (see page 64), and buy a tension gauge when you get really serious. For now, see that the jib halyard is very tight, so you get a good 'twang' when you pluck a shroud.

Mast rake

Mast rake (the fore and aft angle of the mast in the boat) is controlled primarily by the length of the main shrouds (and to a much lesser extent by the jib halyard setting). As a rule of thumb the rake should be about 8 in (20 cm) for the average two-man dinghy. This is measured by setting the boat up level in both fore-and-aft and lateral planes and hanging a heavy weight on the main halyard. The distance between the halyard and lower black band on the mast should be 8 in (20 cm).

The rake of the mast will have an effect on the balance of the boat. A well set up dinghy *when sailed level* should carry slight weather helm. That is, if you let go of the tiller when beating, the boat will steer itself into the wind. If the boat does not do this, or worse still bears away, then more weather helm is required which you can achieve, up to a point, by increasing the rake of the mast.

Above: Measure the mast rake by stretching a tape from the masthead to the transom.
Below: Alternatively, measure between the black band and a plumbline.

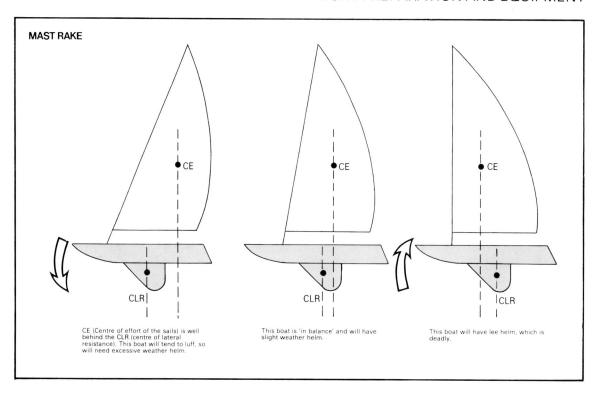

MAST RAKE

CE (Centre of effort of the sails) is well behind the CLR (centre of lateral resistance). This boat will tend to luff, so will need excessive weather helm.

This boat is 'in balance' and will have slight weather helm.

This boat will have lee helm, which is deadly.

Conversely too much weather helm, which needs a large rudder deflection to hold the boat straight and has a slowing effect, can be remedied by moving the mast more upright. You will notice when sailing that too much heel results in excessive weather helm, so always sail the boat as near upright as you can.

Sideways lean

When you have the boat chocked and are checking the mast rake, make sure that the mast isn't leaning over sideways. To do this take the shackle on the main halyard to the base of one shroud, hold it there and cleat the halyard tight. Now move the shackle over to the other shroud; it should touch the base when you pull down with the same tension. If it doesn't, adjust the shroud lengths until the mast is vertical.

Mast bend

Mast bend is a key factor in tuning, and is fully covered in Chapter 9. For the time being angle the spreaders aft until there is a 2 in (5 cm) bend in the middle of the mast: you can judge this by pulling the main halyard tightly down to the gooseneck and judging the distance between the (bent) mast and the (straight) halyard.

Make sure that the spreaders are symmetrical by measuring from the tip of each to the centre of the transom.

Jib fairlead

With the jib set up on land you can check the position of the jib fairlead. The vertical jib sheeting angle is determined by the fore-and-aft position of the fairlead. The jib sheet should approximately bisect the angle of the jib clew.

Below: The line of the jibsheet should roughly bisect the angle of the clew.

Gear and systems

Don't be psyched by boats in the dinghy park that have string and pulleys all over them. You can enter an FD for the Olympic trials next year – but for the time being just make sure that the few *essential* controls are fully adjustable, and that each of these systems works properly.

Mainsheet

Make sure the mainsheet runs freely through its blocks. If you use a ratchet block adjust it so the grip suits you. Make sure the mainsheet cleat angle is right so the sheet can be released quickly when a gust strikes.

Jibsheet

In a similar way, make sure the jib fairleads are smooth and that the cleats are properly angled so the crew doesn't waste time cleating and uncleating the sheet.

Vang (kicking strap)

Once you are sailing this is the primary control for tuning the mainsail. It must be sufficiently powerful to enable you to pull the boom right down when the wind is in the sail. If the class rules allow, the control lines should be divided and led to the helmsman at each side deck.

Jib halyard

The jib halyard usually controls the rig tension, so this system must work one hundred per cent. If you only use a highfield lever it must not be allowed to slip. A more powerful system such as a multi-purchase 16-1 set-up will do the job with a lot less effort on your part.

Check that all the halyard sheaves in the mast are well lubricated. It's surprising how much easier the halyards will run after a squirt of WD40. This is vital for the jib halyard, but the spinnaker halyard must run freely too. Check that the halyards are not twisted round each other in the mast.

The centreboard control

The centreboard also needs an effective control system. When beating you usually want the board fully down – if it comes up of its own accord it can be very annoying. On a reach you will need to raise the board a little. Some quite complicated arrangements can be installed, particularly to raise the board when it is under great side pressure, but to begin with a simple system of retaining it where you want it will be adequate.

The rudder and tiller

You will have either a fixed rudder or one that can be lifted for launching and landing in shallow water. A properly-made fixed rudder has the advantage of complete rigidity and is preferable if you are confident of sailing without a rudder until you reach deep water.

A lifting rudder can be satisfactory, but you will find when fast reaching that the rudder blade will rake aft, giving an unacceptably heavy helm, unless the rudder is fixed in its vertical position by some very positive method. A piece of elastic is just not up to the job. Even a

Below: Two ways of increasing the purchase on the vang – a cascade system of blocks (left) and a lever system (right).

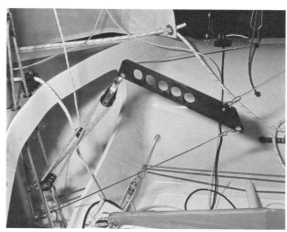

pull-down cord is likely to stretch the quarter-inch or so that will give an unacceptable aft rake. If the class rules allow, by far the best solution is to use a wooden dowel pin or at least a metal split pin to locate it in the fully down position. Wood has the advantage of breaking off if you do ground the rudder unexpectedly; this is preferable to pulling the transom out!

The tiller and tiller extension should also be considered carefully. A positive joint between the tiller and the rudder stock is essential; any slop causes a loss of 'feel'. The best solution is a one-piece arrangement in which tiller and stock are permanently connected together. The extension-to-tiller connection should be of the universal joint variety. (A rubber version is good too, but it needs periodic checking. When a split is noticed, that's your cue to renew it!)

Bailers

Another area of frustration is a leaking bailer. Make certain that the bailers are locked up when you first launch, and then check that no water is seeping in; it is much more difficult to detect a small leak when there is water swilling around in the bottom. If you have a problem it can be almost certainly rectified with a new gasket. Always remember that water is heavy and quite a small amount in the boat will mean you will be carrying lots of unnecessary weight. A bucketful of water weighs about 20 lbs (9 kg). Try pouring a bucketful of water into your boat – it doesn't look a lot.

Carrying a sizeable sponge is to be recommended, particularly on those days when you cannot expect to go fast enough for the self-bailers to work – water has a habit of getting into your boat some way or other even if only from your boots as you climb aboard.

General maintainance

From time to time you should go over your boat with a screwdriver and spanner, checking screws and nuts that may have come loose. In particular, the toestrap screws, the screws or bolts securing the rudder fittings and the fairleads need checking.

It is a very good idea to carry a screwdriver, pair of pliers, knife, shackle, and short lengths of line on your boat at all times. It's surprising how often one of these will come to your rescue.

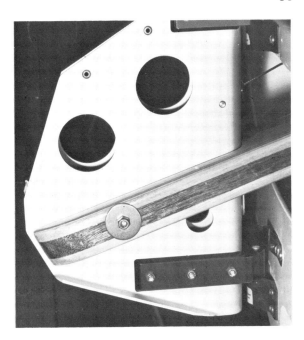

Above: For maximum rigidity this tiller is clamped outside an aluminium rudder head.

Golden rules

★ Keep a checklist *in the boat* of things that don't work.

★ Turn your boat over often to inspect the bottom.

★ Your boat should be light.

★ The shrouds control mast rake.

★ The jib halyard controls rig tension.

★ The jib halyard must be tighter than the forestay.

★ The spreaders control mast bend, as do the chocks at deck level.

★ Mast rake should be about 8 in (20 cm), to give slight weather helm *when the boat is level*.

★ The mast must not lean sideways.

★ All controls *must work*.

★ Keep the boat dry.

★ Check screws and bolts for tightness.

7 Tactics

Tactics are about manoeuvring against other boats. The idea is to position yourself so you have an advantage, and leave your competitors at a disadvantage.

The very presence of your boat will affect the path the wind takes, and you can use this to affect other boats. This is very important since you will often want to slow down an opponent and you will always need to avoid being slowed by someone else.

Wind shadow

Perhaps the most obvious way you can slow a competitor is by taking his wind (blanketing him). On a run the leading boat is very vulnerable to this tactic, since a boat immediately behind can effectively steal her wind. In the diagram the leading boat (A) should luff or gybe to find clean wind.

On a reach the wind shadow comes into effect as a boat overtakes to windward. To prevent this the leeward boat (C) should luff well before the blanketing action begins. The disadvantage of luffing is that you may be forced to sail a much greater distance if the boat behind (D) continues to luff.

Below: 122417 is blanketing 72469 by getting between her and the wind. 72469 will have to drop back or tack to find clear air.

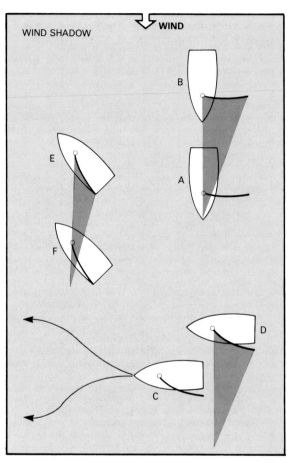

Even when beating there is a wind shadow, although now the cone is much narrower. (Boats E and F.) However, when you are beating an equally important phenomenon comes into effect: dirty wind.

Dirty wind

When beating, your boat not only blankets the area immediately to leeward but it also bends the wind and generally disturbs its smooth path. So when one boat is beating ahead of another, the one behind (G) experiences a heading, cut-up airflow. It is said to be in the *hopeless position*.

In either of the above cases the trailing boat must tack away to seek clean wind.

Lee-bow effect

In this situation the leeward boat (I) is ahead of the wind shadow of the windward boat (J) and is close enough for her sails to bend the wind onto the leeward side of J's sails.

Unless the leeward boat is slower or is being sailed badly she will draw ahead. The weather boat must tack away or she will fall behind.

The leeward boat is said to be in a safe leeward position, and the windward boat is being lee-bowed.

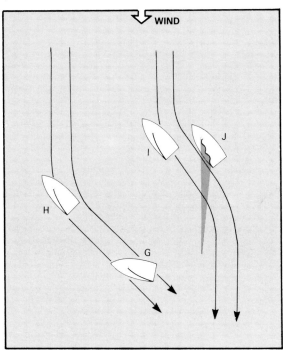

Above: 122417 is lee-bowing 72469, who will soon fall behind.
Below, right to left: A successful luff by 122417 fends off a challenge by 72469.

The start

Unlike a long-distance race in athletics, in yacht racing the sprint comes at the start. Because most races begin on a beat, the boats that are ahead just after the start blanket and lee-bow those behind them. As a result the leaders gradually pull away, so a poor start can cost you the race. And the more boats in a race the more important is a good start and a good position at the first mark.

While it is helpful to cross the start line within two or three seconds of the starting signal and with good speed, the essential thing is to be ahead of the other boats in the immediate vicinity. Also, if the start line is more than 80 ft (25 m) long and not set squarely to the wind, your position on that line is very important.

In championship races where a hundred or more boats are starting, the line may be several hundred metres long. If you start at the wrong end of a line that is biased only five degrees, you have to sail a lot further to the first mark than someone who set off from the favoured end. In the diagram, K will come out ahead of L.

But don't be misled into assuming that, since mark W is closer to the starboard end of the line (as the crow flies), starting at this end will mean you will sail the shortest distance to the mark. As long as the first leg is a beat (so you need to make at least one tack) the position of the windward mark is irrelevant when you're deciding where to start: all that matters is the bias of the startline to the wind. With the wind biased to the port end then the boats starting from that end sail the shorter distance. If the starboard end is favoured then boats beginning at that end should come out ahead.

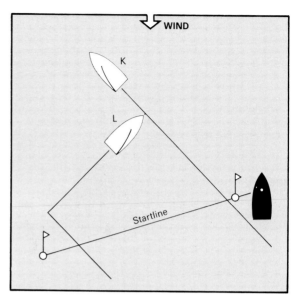

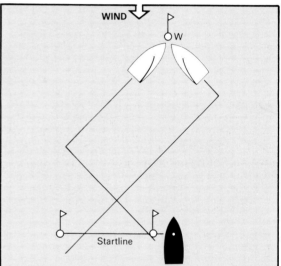

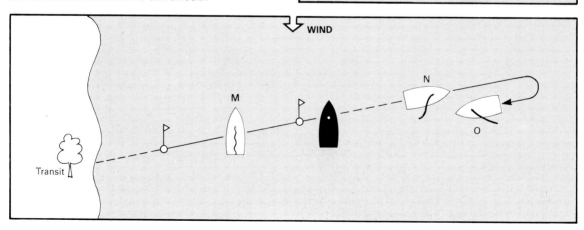

Above: Assessing the line. Letting the jib flap throughout, sail along the extension of the line with half the main flapping (left). Tack, but do not adjust the mainsheet. The main now fills, so the closer end of the line is favoured.

Determining which end of the line is biased

In yachts that are heavy enough to carry way for several seconds when pointed directly into the wind, a judgement can be made by sailing up to the line, luffing until the boom remains on the centreline and then deciding which end of the line your bow is biased towards. In the diagram M's bow points somewhat towards the

Below: For a quick check on the line point the boat head to wind. The bow points towards the favoured end.

committee boat, so that's the end to start.

A very precise method of assessing the line in a light dinghy is to sail your boat along the extension of the line (rather than along the line itself – this is more accurate and the water is less congested). First sail in one direction. Let the jib flap, then ease out the mainsheet until it is half flapping and half drawing (like N in the diagram). Then turn the boat around *without altering the mainsheet's trim* and sail along the extension of the line in the opposite direction. If the sail now fills you are sailing away from the upwind direction (like O). If it luffs more you are pointing towards the upwind direction.

A third method can be used on a dinghy or a yacht, providing there is a compass on board.

Sail close-hauled on port, then on starboard, noting the heading in each case. The wind direction lies mid-way between the two headings. Then sail along the line, or better still its extension, and determine its bearing. Usually it will *not* be at 90 degrees to the wind direction, and it is now a relatively simple matter to work out which end of the line is upwind. The disadvantage of this method is that it can take some time, and if the wind is shifting or the line is changed (it can be moved anytime before the five-minute gun) you may not have the time.

Having determined if one end of the line is favoured your next decision is where on the line you should start. In the absence of other factors, such as wanting to go a particular way up the first beat, then try to start at or near the biased end of the line.

Using a stopwatch

Most books tell you to start your stopwatch at the five minute signal, check it at the four, then count down to the start. In practice this is impossible, because you don't know when the five minute signal is going to be made.

By all means start the watch at the five minute signal (you'll be a bit late). Plan your manoeuvring so you are near the committee boat with four-and-a-half minutes to go, and then zero your watch. You should be able to hear the officer of the day (OOD) counting down, and you can then get the timing exactly.

If you have a watch with both a stopwatch and a timer mode, use the stopwatch for the first half minute, then flip to timer just before the four minute signal and hit it right on the button.

Note that the four minute signal is the key – if there's any discrepancy you assume the four minute signal was correct, not the five. You are not racing until the four minute signal.

Starting mid-line

If the fleet is large aim to start a little way from the extreme ends; there should be more room near the middle. Try to approach the line with sails flapping on a close reach for the last minute (more if it is a very big fleet) being particularly careful to avoid dropping down on boats to leeward who have the right of way. Luff boats to weather and attempt to create space to leeward so that you can bear off a little with about 15 seconds to go and hit the line at some speed. If you just sheet in with five seconds to go and everyone around you is moving they will leave you for dead.

Judging how far you are behind the line is difficult in a large fleet, and you need to keep up with the first rank of starters, yet not be so far forward that you will be spotted as a premature starter.

Even when you can see both ends of the line it is difficult to judge whether you are on it or not unless you are near one end. In fact you always think you are over well before you are actually on the line. Have you ever noticed that when you finish a race the race committee always seems to be late in giving you a finishing signal? In fact they're not – it's just that you think you're on the line well before you are.

This is how to judge accurately your distance from the line. You remember you're supposed to be reaching up and down the extension of the line assessing the bias? At the same time look for a distant object in line with the end of the starting line. This is your transit (N has found a tree to serve this purpose). When you're approaching the line to start, move forwards until the appropriate end lines up with your transit once more.

At this point you will know that you are right on the line. You will probably be surprised at how far forward you can go, but you will learn to trust your transit (provided the boat marking the end of the line isn't drifting!) A transit beyond the port end is best, but if nothing is visible a transit the other way will do. As you make your start keep the transit in mind. Until it begins to line up with the mark there is no need to begin holding back.

Above: Take a transit on the startline – here the end of the trees lines up with the ODM.

Another useful and quick way of determining if you are still behind the line is the 'tiller method'. Sail along the line, point your bow at one end of the line, centre your tiller and look back along it. If the tiller is pointing back behind the other end of the line then you are still behind the line. If the tiller is pointing 'over' the line you're over. This method is more revealing than you might imagine. Try it out!

Remember good starts can be vital. Knowing how close you are to the line when others don't is extremely useful.

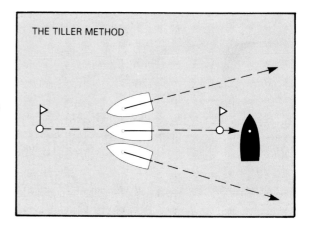

THE TILLER METHOD

Above: Sight along the tiller to check that you are behind the line.

How do I make a starboard-end start?

Sail slowly, and as close to the wind as possible, so you reach the windward end of the line with the gun. Boats to windward have no rights and are forced out. Boats to leeward can't touch you – you are already sailing as close to the wind as possible.

How do I make a port-end start?

Aim to be at the port end of the line with two minutes to go. Reach towards the fleet which will be sitting on the line, flapping, about 100

metres away. Tack just before the first boat, then sail as slowly as possible towards the port end of the line. With ten seconds to go sheet in and cross the line at full speed.

The gate start

For some years now gate starts have been used as an alternative at large championships. The success of this radical system can be measured by the number of otherwise conservative classes that have adopted it.

How it works

The gate start is a dynamic starting method. This is to say that the starting line is changing all the time as boats in their turn begin to race. At its simplest, one chosen competitor (the pathfinder) sails on port tack across the whole fleet, followed by a motor boat (the gate launch). Each boat starts in turn under the gate launch's stern. In this way each boat will have a start equal to everyone else, so long as each boat just clears the launch's stern, and the pathfinder and gate launch travel at a constant speed and direction while the gate is opening (that is to say, the wind stays steady in both strength and direction).

If a significant change in wind strength or direction takes place the race committee should abandon the start, but smaller changes can be tolerated and still give a much fairer start than can be reasonably expected from a conventional line start.

A championship gate start is rather more complicated than described above, but the principle is the same.

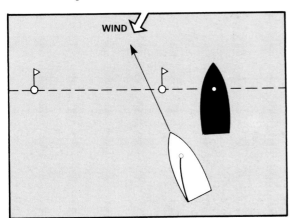

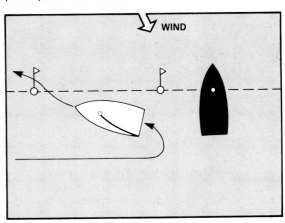

Above: A fleet of Solings in a gate start. The pathfinder (right) leads the small gate launch while the larger boat acts as a guard launch.

The procedure

The starting signals are made from a separate committee boat. Approximately 15 seconds before the start signal is due the pathfinder, followed closely by the gate launch, proceeds on a close-hauled port tack away from the vicinity of the committee boat. Three seconds before the start a free-floating buoy is dropped from the stern of the gate launch. At the starting signal boats may sail across the imaginary line between the centre of the gate launch and the centre of the floating buoy. In addition to the gate launch there is usually another powered craft (the guard launch) which positions herself level with and to leeward of the pathfinder and protects her from any collisions with wayward yachts not obeying the rules. This entourage continues for approximately two to three minutes before the pathfinder is given permission to tack or continue as she sees fit. After the pathfinder has tacked off the gate launch will continue at the same speed and on the same course for a further minute or so before stopping and floating for approximately a further minute and signalling the closing of the gate. These times may be shortened when a smaller fleet is being started.

Techniques of gate starting

Various decisions need to be taken as to how to start. Should you go early or late? This will depend on a number of considerations.

Is the pathfinder likely to be faster on the beat than you? Since she is usually the boat that finished tenth in the previous race, if you are a beginner then going late will probably be to your advantage.

Also strategical considerations such as which way you want to go up the beat will determine when to go. If you expect the wind to veer (move in a clockwise direction) going late will pay off – or vice versa if you think it will back. The current may also affect your decision.

Once you have decided where you will start, you need to put yourself in a position to make a good approach. The best way to do this is to sail close-hauled on port tack away from the committee boat area for a predetermined time, say two to two-and-a-half minutes if you choose to start late. You are following the course that the pathfinder will sail. Now bear off onto a broad reach for another minute, then tack and stop with your sails flapping. You are now approximately one to one-and-a-half minutes of starboard-tack beating from your start, if the wind is steady. However, you should expect to take at least twice this time to cover the distance as you slowly close-reach towards the gate boat.

This is the critical time where good technique pays dividends. You know from your watch when the start is due. You may not see the pathfinder at the moment the gun goes if you are starting late. However, you should soon spot the entourage of pathfinder, gate launch, guard

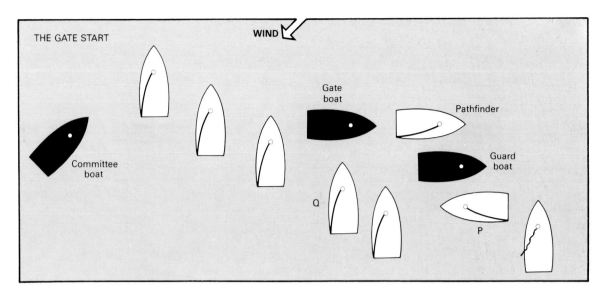

THE GATE START

WIND

Gate boat

Pathfinder

Guard boat

Committee boat

Q

P

boat and gaggle of starters proceeding along their course. Once you have seen them, make sure you are always well forward of the position that will enable you to reach them at full speed.

Remember it will be easy to slow up by easing sheets and luffing, virtually to a halt if necessary. Never, never be panicked into bearing off because you are worried that you may arrive too early. This will only speed you up and ensure that you *do* arrive early. You will also hit the boats to leeward, as boat P in the diagram is about to discover.

As with a conventional start try to maintain a gap to leeward by 'holding up' competitors to weather of you, so that as you approach the gate boat you can bear off, gain speed and start close under her stern with full speed. Q is doing this. Remember the gate boat is moving so don't aim for her stern but rather further forward. Just keep your eyes open and you won't hit her or anyone to leeward. However, any collision with the pathfinder, gate boat or guard boat will result in instant disqualification, so do watch it!

Tactics on on the beat

Your speed will be low if you are in someone's windshadow, or if there is another boat dead ahead or lee-bowing you. If this is the case, look over your shoulder to see if you are clear to tack. If you have room, tack immediately, but if there is a pile of boats to weather you may have to carry on for a bit. Sometimes it pays to bear

away a little or even slow down to let them by, then tack into clear air.

Since you have made a poor start, tack onto port and duck the whole fleet. (Since they are almost in line at this stage, you will only lose a length or two.) Once in clear air, tack back onto starboard.

Port v starboard

There will be many times on the beat when you find yourself on a collision course with a boat on the opposite tack.

If you are on port tack you must keep clear, but you can choose whether you bear away behind your rival (don't forget to ease the sheets a bit, to make this easier) or tack shortly before you hit her. The rules require you to complete your tack

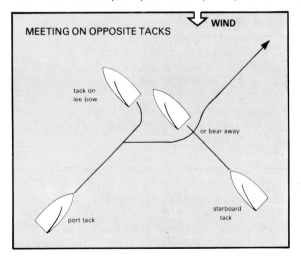

MEETING ON OPPOSITE TACKS

WIND

tack on lee bow

or bear away

port tack

starboard tack

a short distance away from the starboard tack boat; she must have time to avoid you, beginning her avoiding action no earlier than the time you completed your tack. Note that if you tack at just the right moment, you may end up lee-bowing your opponent. But if you get it wrong, she may hit you or sail over the top of you. Sailing's like that.

If you are on starboard you have right of way. However, power confers responsibility: you must keep a straight course so that the port-tack boat has a chance to keep clear. Even if there is a windshift, you must keep going in a straight line until she is clear of you.

When ahead

It is a general principle that if you are ahead of another boat, and want to stay there, keep between her and the next mark. She then has to sail around your hull to pass you, which means she is not only sailing further but is doing so in your wake. That should keep her back!

On a beat this tactic is even more effective because you can hold the rival boat in your windshadow. If you're really determined to keep her behind you can *cover*. This involves staying on her wind by tacking every time she does. But be careful – covering slows you down and other boats can sneak by while you're duelling.

Tactics on the reach

The quickest way down the reach is a straight line from one mark to the next. However, if your rivals let you sail this course, you're lucky! The problem is that overtaking boats (R) push up to

Above, right to left: 122417 is asking for trouble approaching the windward mark on port. She must give way to 72469 who is on starboard, and must not tack too close. In the event she hits 72469 while still tacking, and must retire (or do a 720-degree turn).

windward. The boats to leeward (S) get nervous about their wind being stolen and steer high also. The result is that everyone sails an enormous arc (X), losing ground on the leaders.

You have to decide whether or not to go on the 'great circle'; the alternative is to sail a leeward path (Y). You have to go down far enough to avoid the blanketing effect of the boats to windward – but usually you will sail a shorter distance than they do. You will also get

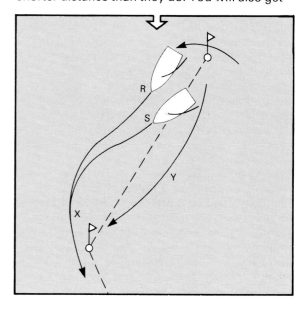

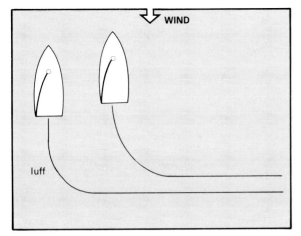

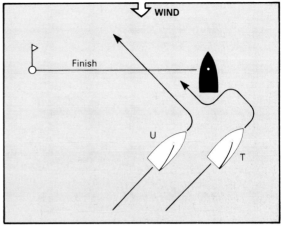

the inside turn at the gybe mark. You can go for the leeward route on the second reach too, but this time you will be on the outside at the turn.

To protect your wind you are allowed to luff, that is turn towards the wind, giving the windward boat time to keep clear. You can go right up to head to wind, and the windward boat has to keep clear. Usually, a little luff in good time will prevent someone behind from trying to roll over you.

You can continue to luff until the overlap is broken (until the line through the windward boat's transom is ahead of you).

If you are doing the overtaking, work well to windward before you try to get through another boat's wind. You then have plenty of time to see the luff coming, and keep clear.

Tactics on the run

Your 'ideal' course to the leeward mark is often impossible in the presence of other boats. If another boat is blanketing you (if her burgee is pointing straight at your mast) luff a little into clear air. If she continues to blanket you, and you don't want to veer off course too far, then gybe so as to go for clear air on the other side. You can easily gybe back later.

If you find yourself behind another boat you can of course blanket her. Simply sail right up behind (blanketing is effective at four mast lengths, but becomes deadly as you get even nearer) and swerve to one side at the last moment. Passing to leeward is often the best, as she is then unable to luff you. And it's an especially good choice if it gives you the inside turn at the leeward mark.

Tactics at the finish

If you have one boat close behind, cover her to the finish.

If you're level-pegging with one or more boats try to avoid the position of T in the diagram: you can't tack for the line until U does and you'll come in behind her. Try to manoeuvre yourself into the controlling position, and hold well on until you are certain to lay your end of the finish line. That's really flaunting your tactical advantage.

Golden rules

★ Avoid being blanketed.

★ Avoid the hopeless position.

★ Avoid being lee-bowed.

★ Start near the forward (upwind) end of the startline.

★ Ignore the position of the windward mark when deciding where to start (provided the first leg is a beat).

★ Keep in the front rank before the start.

★ Take a transit so you know when you're on the line.

★ Keep between your opponent and the next mark.

★ Offwind, keep your wind clear and try to sail straight for the next mark.

8 Strategy

In the absence of other boats there will often be a preferred way to go on the beat, reach or run. Quite often the strategic factors outweigh the tactical ones; for instance it may well be necessary to start at the downwind end of the line in order to sail into a favourable current.

Short beats

If the first beat is short, as is often the case when racing inland, it will be too risky to start at the port end of the line if there are a number of boats in the race. A short beat means that most of the fleet will arrive at the windward mark at the same time. It is far safer to approach this mark with right of way on starboard tack rather than risk coming in on port looking for a gap which may not exist. It is also advisable to overstand the mark slightly. You are likely to be approaching the mark on starboard behind other boats and the disturbed air will reduce your pointing ability alarmingly.

The most important strategic considerations are variation of wind strength and direction, and tidal current. Before the start of a race it is essential to take account of the prevailing conditions on the course and work out how they are going to affect you on the beat and, later, on the downwind legs.

Current

It is an advantage to sail in the area where the current is strongest when it's with you and where it's weakest when it's against you.

Where the port side of the first beat is favoured you can start wherever the tactical considerations dictate, then continue on starboard tack towards the left side of the course. If the starboard side of the course is best then you may have to start at or towards that end, in order to be able to tack after the start and go that way.

Determining the direction of the current

It isn't always easy to know which way the current is flowing. Here are a few pointers.

Before each race, find out the times of high and low water and write them on your boat with a chinagraph pencil.

Look at a chart or tidal atlas to see which way the tide will be going during the race. Draw a picture on your boat to remind you.

If you expect the tide to turn during the race, set the alarm on your watch to go off half an hour before. This will remind you to look out for the tidal change.

Once on the racecourse you need to see if the tidal predictions are correct. In fact tides are affected by barometric pressure and wind, so don't expect the published data to be precise.

- Look at moored boats. Since they are usually anchored at the bow, they swing with the tidal flow.

- Sail near a buoy whenever you get the chance and look to see if there is a swirl past it.

- If in doubt, drop a half-empty beer can near a fixed object (a buoy or a post) and see which way it drifts. Be sure to retrieve the can after use – you may need it again!

Determining when the tide turns

- Expect the tide to turn roughly when the published data predicts.

- Watch anchored boats to see when they swing.

- Wind-against-tide causes larger waves than wind-with-tide. So watching the sea state gives a tidal clue.

- Watch the flow past buoys.

Where is the current strongest?

Water is slowed down by friction (with the bottom or the shore). It also tends to flow in a straight line unless forced to bend. It follows that

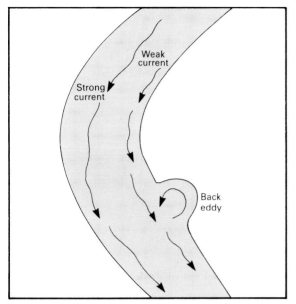

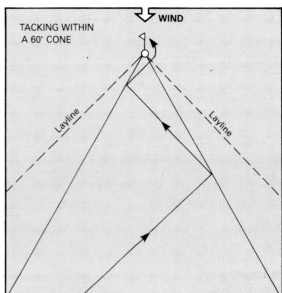

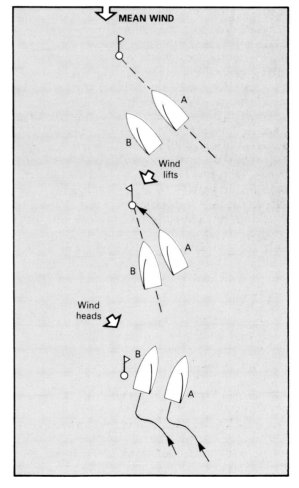

the strongest current is in deep water, such as the middle of a channel, and round the outside of bends. In bays there may even be back eddies.

Naturally you will try to sail in the weakest current when the flow is against you, and in the strongest current when the flow is with you. When sailing against the tide:

- Keep inshore.

- Keep in shallow water.

- Go for the inside of bends.

- Head for bays.

Do the opposite when the tide is with you.

General strategy on the beat

In the absence of windshifts or current variations, tack within a 60-degree cone. Note that your tacks get more frequent as you approach the weather mark. Under no circumstances should you approach either layline, because if the wind shifts you will find yourself either overstanding or sailed across. In the diagram boat A is on the layline, comfortably ahead of boat B. If the wind lifts A has overstood and B reaches the mark first. If the wind heads neither can lay the mark and both should tack. Once again, B comes out ahead.

Windshifts and windbends

A windshift occurs when the direction of the wind suddenly alters.

A windbend is a gradual, permanent bending of the wind over a large area of water.

You need to take account of variations in wind direction, though they are not as predictable as current variations and therefore not as reliable. If wind and current demand different sides of the course, and the decision is finely balanced, go for the best current every time.

Compass sailing

The only reliable way to spot windshifts and bends is with a compass. Here is how to use it.

Before the start, beat on starboard tack. Keep the front of the jib just lifting all the time and watch the compass numbers moving behind the line on the case '270, 275, 270, 265, 270, 270' you say to yourself. It's obvious that the wind is averaging 270, so write this by the compass. Now sail on, and watch to see if the bearing alters.

In a shifting wind you might expect readings like this: 270, 280, 280, 280, 270, 260, 260, 260, 270. . . . The wind has swung right (veered) 10 degrees, then swung left (backed) 10 degrees. We will see later that you can tack on these shifts with advantage. For now try to find the period of the shifts – do they swing every minute, or every half-minute?

In a windbend you would expect the readings to alter gradually (and you'd expect the bend to be there on the next lap, too). '270, 275, 280, 285, 290, 295. . . .'

Having sorted the readings on starboard, tack and repeat the exercise on port. Write down the mean wind there too, and the limits of its wanderings. Then when you're actually racing you've got a lot of background wind information to go on.

Using windshifts

Short-term windshifts are caused by two principal effects:

1 As the wind flows around obstacles such as buildings and islands it becomes turbulent and inconsistent in direction.

2 The wind at higher altitudes always blows in a different direction from the wind at sea level. Under certain conditions chunks of this high air come down to sea level. The new air is not

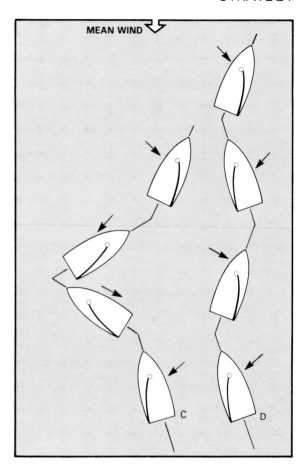

only moving faster but is going in a different direction from the prevailing wind, so you are hit by a shifting gust.

Some of the shifts are more pronounced and last longer than others – it is these that you have to spot and use.

In shifty winds, stay close to the middle of the beat. Tack each time the wind heads you (forces you to alter course *away* from the mark). In the diagram, boat C takes no account of windshifts. Note how little progress it makes to windward compared with boat D which tacks each time the wind heads it.

The main problem is to differentiate between a real shift and a short-lived change in the wind. For that reason, sail on into each shift for five or ten seconds to make sure it's going to last. If a header lasts that long, tack.

If you find yourself tacking too often, or are confused, sail on one tack for a while until you're sure what the wind is doing. Remember that you

usually lose at least a boat's length each time
you tack, so there always has to be a good
reason to do so.

Using windbends
Permanent windbends are often caused by a land
mass upwind of you. In the diagram the curved
shoreline is causing the bend. Always sail
towards the centre of a bend (like E in the
diagram). In that way you are lifted on both tacks.

One-sided beats

If the course has been badly laid, or there has
been a permanent windshift, the beat will be
one-sided. (You will sail longer on one tack than
the other).
   In this case always sail the long tack first. Then
if the wind shifts even further, you may be able
to lay the mark without tacking at all. If it stays
steady you lose nothing. If it swings back
towards the old direction, you are already on the
favoured side of the course: tack, and sail across
the opposition on the new lifted tack.

Watch the other boats
At the beginning of the first beat ask your crew
to pick one boat of your standard that is going
right and one that is going left. At the windward
mark, check which came out ahead. This will
give you a clue as to which side of the beat paid
off.
   Repeat on each beat. If you reckon the same
side is paying every time, go that way. But if the
evidence is inconclusive, stick to the 60-degree
cone.

Strategy on the reach

The shortest distance is a direct line between the
two marks and many boat lengths can be lost by
steering an erratic or curved course down the
reach.
   When you are sailing across a current it is
useful to find a transit on the shore beyond the
next mark (or otherwise one on the shore behind
the previous mark) to help you stay on the
rhumb line. Simply pointing the bow at the mark
will ensure that you sail a long curve as the
current sweeps you off course. When the current
is taking you upwind of the rhumb line you will,

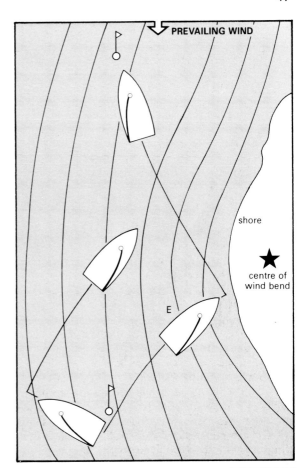

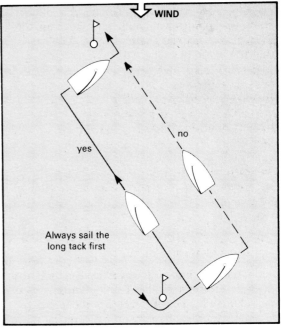

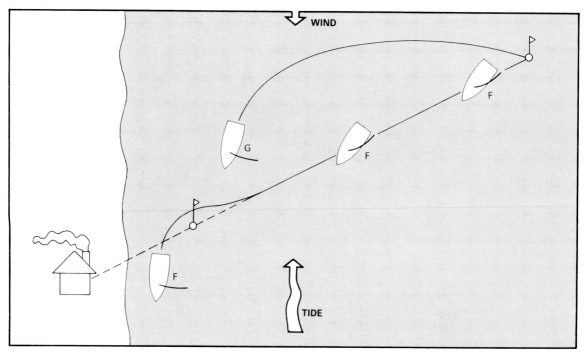

by steering low (like F), gain enormously over the unwary (like G) who will end up running back towards the mark against the tide. They will slow dramatically; meanwhile you will storm through them on a reach, and round the buoy well ahead.

In general, luff as the wind drops, and bear away quickly as it increases. In this way you meet each gust sooner and stay with it longer. If you need to bear away, try to choose a header: you will then lose no speed and can luff again when the wind frees once more.

The run

In many boats – particularly those with spinnakers (and of course all catamarans) – the fastest course on a running leg will not be the rhumb line but one that takes advantage of the extra speed of a broad reach. So long as the speed gain more than offsets the extra distance you need to travel, then gybing downwind will pay. Because it is a mirror image of the beat, this process is often called (perhaps rather confusingly) tacking downwind. The trick is to know how much to aim up from the rhumb line. In general the lighter the wind the more you should head up. On average you will find that your best course is 10 degrees off the dead run.

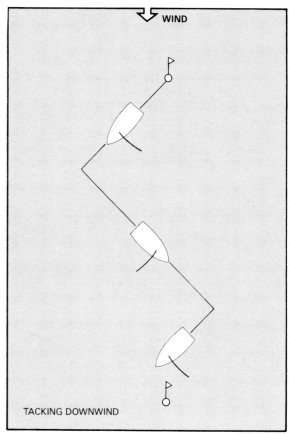

TACKING DOWNWIND

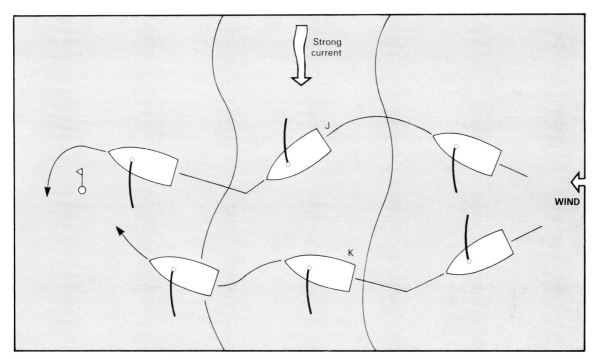

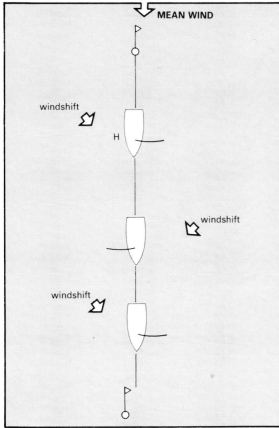

Gybing on shifts and on the tide

If the run is not true, choose the gybe that heads nearest the mark. (This is similar to choosing the long tack first, when beating.) Then if the wind heads, you will simply speed up. If it frees, you can gybe.

As on the beat, windshifts can be used with advantage on the run. The idea is to keep at a constant angle to the wind. As it heads you bear away – that's great, you're now pointing more directly towards the mark. If it lifts you will need to sail further off the rhumb line to keep up speed, and should gybe so as to sail more directly down the rhumb line. Note how H gybes on each shift and sails fast straight to the leeward mark.

If you think the wind is going to shift a short way down the run (your experience on the beat will give this away) then initially choose the direction that will allow you to gybe when the wind shifts (and then point directly at the mark on a broad reach).

If there is an uneven current or tide across the course, choose to cross the strongest tide on the gybe that gives the most advantage. J crosses the strong tide on port; the tide pushes her sail through the air, and 'squirts' her forward. K does the opposite, and her sail backs in the strong tidal region.

The finish

Many places can be lost by finishing at the wrong end of the line if it is significantly biased. Remember, it will be quicker to reach the downwind end – the opposite end to the one you would aim to start from! The best way to judge this at the end of the last beat is by sailing on a layline towards one end. Let's say you're on port tack just laying the starboard end of the line. As you cross the other layline you can judge which is the shorter distance to the finish. In the diagram the pin end is favoured, so tack and finish by the buoy.

   If the line was already set on the previous round and the wind direction is relatively steady you assess the situation on the penultimate lap and make your plans in advance.

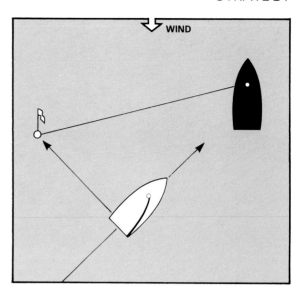

Golden rules

★ On a short beat keep to the right-hand side of the course.

★ Find out which way the current or tide is flowing.

★ Head for deep water and the outside of bends when the tide is with you.

★ If everything is equal, tack up a 60-degree cone.

★ STAY WELL INSIDE THE LAYLINES.

★ Use your compass to spot windshifts.

★ Tack on headers.

★ Sail towards the centre of windbends.

★ On a one-sided beat, sail the long leg first.

★ When sailing cross-tide, point into the tide and use a transit to sail a straight course 'over the land'.

★ Gybe on windshifts.

★ Choose the gybe that takes you most directly to the leeward mark.

★ Keep strong tide under your lee bow.

★ Go for the downwind end of the finish line.

9 Tuning

Some boats are faster than others, even when they are one-designs. This difference is often called boatspeed. Boatspeed is great when you've got it: as the man said, 'Boatspeed makes you a tactical genius'.

A friend who is a racing driver was amazed at the effort we put in to speed up from, say, 6 knots to 6.1 knots. He was more interested in getting up to 200 mph! Yet if you were going 0.1 knots faster you'd be 300 yards or metres further up the fleet by the finish; this difference might well be magnified still further, because the leading boats slow up those behind.

So why do good crews have better boatspeed? The answer is that they can recognise a slow boat and do something about it. The beginner is never sure whether it's the boat or his technique that's wrong. But do bear in mind that you can almost always improve your technique more than you can improve the boat. It's only when you're looking for the last fraction of a per cent that you need to start spending money.

General requirements

Let's suppose that you're relatively happy with your technique and are on the boatspeed trail. The first thing to do is . . . enjoy it! Tuning is largely trial and error, yet more rubbish is talked about it than any other aspect of sailing. There is no point in slavishly following some set formula; you're more likely to get good speed by having fun playing around with different settings.

Having said that, there's no point in trying to tune a badly-prepared boat (see Chapter 6). Your sails must be in good condition too: one season's use is maximum if you want to win a national championship, two seasons for a club series. It's a sad fact of life that cloth does deteriorate with use, and flapping causes the finish to break down.

Finally, it is impossible to tune a boat unless you're sailing her *upright*. Any discernable heel will affect the balance; all dinghies are designed to be sailed upright.

What are we trying to do?

All boats are tuned for the beat. (Having got them right for upwind work, all you have to do offwind is to make the sails fuller, and perhaps rake the mast forward).

The main objective is to be able to adjust the curve (belly) in the sails for the wind strength. You want maximum fullness (which gives maximum power) in medium winds. As the breeze builds, you need to gradually flatten the sails to reduce their power – otherwise you'll be unable to hold the boat up. Surprisingly, you need quite quite flat sails in light airs, too, because the feeble breeze is incapable of bending around highly-curved sails.

The mainsail is cut with a curved luff. When this is set on a straight mast, fullness is forced into the sail. To remove the fullness, simply bend the mast: when the curve in the mast matches the curve in the luff, the sail will be almost flat. (Not quite flat, because some curve is also built into the sail by curving the edges of the panels.) The main aim here is to match the mast bend to the luff curve – if the mast over-bends at any point, horrible creases form from that point.

The jib is not set on a mast, but the front edge is controlled in a similar way via rig tension. Sloppy rigging puts curve into the front of the jib, while tight rigging pulls the jib luff straight and gets rid of fullness. In general, about 350 lbs tension on the jib luff wire is a good starting point.

One more objective is to balance the helm. With the boat beating in a medium breeze, and upright, there should be a very slight pull on the tiller. (This is weather helm.) Too much weather helm is bad because the rudder is then going through the water at an angle, which slows the boat down. But lee helm is disastrous, because the flow of water over the rudder forces the boat to leeward. Never rig a boat for lee helm.

What do all the controls do?

Shrouds   The shrouds control mast rake. If you shorten the shrouds, you rake the mast aft; if you make them longer you reduce the aft rake.

Jib halyard   The jib halyard pulls the mast up tight against the pull of the shrouds; in other words tightening the jib halyard increases tension. The primary aim here is to stop the luff of the jib sagging, as this forces fullness into the front of the sail and stops you pointing. A secondary effect of rig tension is that it allows the spreaders to control mast bend.

Jib fairlead   The position of the jib fairlead controls the slot (the gap between the jib and the mainsail). If the slot is narrow, the rig is powered up; if it's wide the rig is depowered. There are three ways of moving the fairlead – fore-and-aft, up-and-down and side-to-side. Moving the fairlead *forward, down* and *in* all close the slot and increase power.

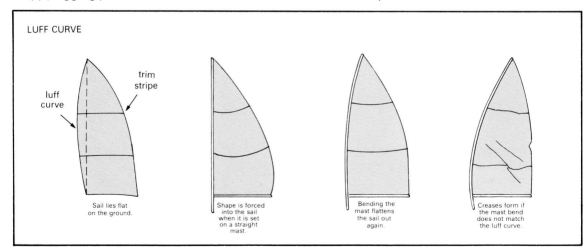

LUFF CURVE

trim stripe

luff curve

Sail lies flat on the ground.

Shape is forced into the sail when it is set on a straight mast.

Bending the mast flattens the sail out again.

Creases form if the mast bend does not match the luff curve.

Above and right: When the jib barber hauler (above) is pulled down the jib becomes fuller and the leech tighter (right). This powers up the jib but may backwind the main. Letting it up does the opposite (far right).

Jib sheet The tension on this is critical. A tight sheet gives a flat sail with a hard leech, while a loose sheet gives the opposite. The difference between tight and loose is only about 2 in (5 cm), so it's best to mark the sheet at its optimum position. You can find this by sighting the sail from behind, and adjusting the fairlead and sheet until the leech of the jib is parallel to the closest part of the main.

Spreaders The spreaders control the bend in the middle of the mast. Raking the spreaders aft bows the middle of the mast forwards; raking the spreaders forward straightens the mast again. Lengthening the spreaders stiffens the mast sideways; shortening the spreaders lets the middle of the mast bow to windward, which is a (rather dubious) way of depowering the rig.

The rake of the spreaders is usually measured as the distance from the back of the mast to a straight line across the spreader tips (see photo).

Mast ram Mast rams are only fitted on boats where the mast passes through the deck and is stepped on the hog. The ram controls mast bend low down. If you release the ram (or remove chocks) the mast automatically bows forwards, while tensioning the ram (or adding chocks) pushes the mast aft and stiffens it.

Kicking strap (vang) The kicker (vang) pulls both down *and* forwards. The downwards pull helps prevent the leech of the main twisting, provided the boom is stiff (otherwise the boom bends and the effect is lost). The forwards pull presses the boom against the mast which bends forwards (unless the ram is tensioned).

Below: With the vang released (left) the mast straightens and the mainsail leech opens. If it is tightened (right) the effect is reversed.

Above: The mainsheet tightens the leech of the main and powers it up (left). Reducing tension (right) opens the leech, reducing power.

Mainsheet The mainsheet allows the boom to swing in and out. But once the boom is on the centreline, increasing mainsheet tension pulls down on the boom, which in turn tightens the leech. This is a similar effect to that of the kicking strap (vang), but if the sheet take-off points on the boom are vertically above the traveller you

Above: The traveller alters the angle of the main to the centreline, while the set of the sail remains constant.

can tighten the leech of the main without bending the mast.

Cunningham The cunningham tensions the luff of the main, which pulls the fullness forward, ruining your pointing ability in light and medium winds. It also removes the creases near the luff. The cunningham also slackens the leech of the

Below: Cunningham tension (left) opens the top of the leech and removes creases in the luff. Less tension closes the leech (right).

Below: Tightening the outhaul reduces depth in the foot of the sail (left). Loosening it gives a full foot but a tighter lower leech (right).

main, so in practise it is only used when you're overpowered. Ignore those creases: they don't really slow you down much.

Outhaul   The outhaul stretches the foot of the main. Tensioning it reduces the draft in the foot of the sail and stops the leech just above the boom curling to windward. Both effects are admirable when beating, so always have the outhaul tight to windward. Let it off on the reach and the run to give a baggy sail.

Initial set-up onshore

You need first to get the mast in roughly the right position. You can do this on land, with the mainsail *down*.

Hoist the jib and pull the halyard really tight. If you have a tension meter test the jib luff tension: it should be about 350 lbs (160 kg). If not, it should give a satisfying twang when plucked.

Sight up the mast. There should be no sideways bend. Take the end of the halyard to each chain plate to check the mast isn't leaning to one side.

Sight up the mast again, while pulling the main halyard tight between the top of the mast and the gooseneck. There should be a reasonable, progressive bend: 2-4 inches (5-10 cm) is a sensible place to start.

The rake of the mast is measured by fixing a tape measure to the main halyard, running it up to the top of the mast, and measuring to the centre of the top of the transom. Try to get an expert to give you his rake figures, then copy them. For example, on a 470 the rake should be 22 ft 2 in (6·76 m) for light winds, progressing to 21 ft 10 in (6·65 m) for strong winds.

Failing this, put the boat on the water and hang a heavy weight (such as a toolbox) from the main halyard. Measure the distance from the halyard to the back of the mast at gooseneck level: about 8 in (20 cm) is a good starting point.

Initial set-up on water

Now for the fun bit!

Choose a day with a medium wind and fairly flat water, rig the boat and get her sailing properly on a beat. Remember to keep the hull flat throughout this exercise.

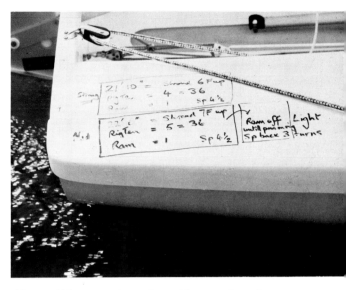

Above: When you have found fast settings for the rig, record them – as here, on the deck of a 470 belonging to one of the authors.

Pull in the mainsheet almost as hard as you can with one hand. Your mainsail should set nicely. If there are horrible creases coming out of the centre of the mast, reduce the mast bend by tensioning the ram and/or raking the spreaders forwards. But if you can't get creases by pulling really hard on the mainsheet, increase the mast bend.

Now let go of the tiller. If the boat is flat, she should luff very slowly. If she luffs hard, you have weather helm and need either to rake the mast forward, move it forward bodily (with the same rake), loosen the leech of the main by bending the mast, rake the centreboard aft or move the centreboard pivot aft.

If the boat bears away when you let go of the tiller, you have lee helm. This is disastrous, so rake the mast back, move it aft at the foot, tighten the leech by straightening the mast, rake the centreboard forward or move the centreboard pivot forward.

Adjusting the rig for various windstrengths

Each class is different, but here are a few general pointers to tweaking for various windstrengths.

- As the wind builds, the kicking strap (vang) should be pulled tighter.

- When the wind is light let off the ram to bend the mast. In medium winds the mast needs to be fairly straight for maximum power. As you become overpowered, gradually bend the mast more by letting off the ram once again to flatten the sail.

- In light winds ease the mainsheet slightly, with the vang slack. In medium winds pull it tight. In strong winds ease the mainsheet again (with tight vang).

- The mast should be gradually raked back as the wind increases. This reduces the overlap between jib and main, thereby depowering the rig. This does not increase weather helm, because the mainsheet will be eased in these conditions.

- In strong winds raise the centreboard or daggerboard a little. When a gust hits, the boat slides sideways instead of tripping over the centreboard and heeling excessively.

Golden rules

★ You can always improve your technique more than you can improve your boat.

★ Tune your boat for the beat.

★ Mast bend controls sail shape.

★ The shrouds control rake.

★ The jib halyard controls rig tension.

★ Raking the spreaders aft bends the mast.

★ Use the cunningham only when overpowered.

★ Tension the outhaul when beating.

The adjustments to make as you go 'through the gears' are summed up in the following table.

	Mainsheet	Vang	Cunningham	Outhaul	Rig Tension	Jib fairlead
Light	Eased	Eased	Eased	Tight	Tight	Down (or forward)
Medium	Tight	Medium	Eased	Eased two inches	Tight	Down (or forward)
Strong	Eased	Very tight	Tight	Tight	Tighter or eased depending on class	Up (or aft)

10   The spinnaker

The spinnaker adds great interest to downwind sailing, particularly for your crew. It adds excitement and tactical interest to the run, gives power on the reach and puts a premium on good gybing technique.

Spinnaker gear

In a dinghy, the spinnaker is usually set from just above the jib, and the sheets are led outside all the sails to blocks well aft in the boat. A spinnaker pole is attached to the weather corner (the tack) which helps to stabilise the spinnaker and, on the run, increases the width exposed to the wind. The pole setting also affects the general shape of the sail. (It is illegal according to the racing rules to fly a spinnaker for any length of time without the pole, or to pole the sail out on the leeward side.)

   The line from the pole corner is called the guy, while the other line is the sheet. A twinning line or hook is used to pull down the guy, keeping it out of the crew's way and keeping the pull of the guy at the correct angle. An uphaul and downhaul control the vertical angle of the pole.

   It is more important that all the spinnaker gear works 100 per cent than any of the other equipment because a problem in raising or lowering can lose you a huge distance. Ensure that the pole end fittings work effectively and will only release the sheet or guy when required.

The pole and controls
The pole uphaul and downhaul systems should be positive, only relying on elastic to retract the arrangement when the pole is taken down. If your class rules allow it, the pole should be stowed along the boom, from where it can be quickly and easily set by the crew.

The sheet and guy
Use non-stretch rope for the sheet and guy. The leads should be as far aft and as far outboard as possible to open the leech of the kite and reduce backwinding of the mainsail.

The halyard
Quick setting of the spinnaker can be achieved when you haven't a chute by fitting a pump system. This is a multi-purchase halyard that works in reverse: as you pull upwards the halyard moves double or triple the distance you pull. Two pumps should be enough to raise the kite completely.

Raising and lowering the spinnaker

A great deal of time, and consequently speed can be lost during setting and lowering of the

spinnaker. In particular, setting the kite at the beginning of a close reach can cost you a lot of time. The sail must go up as quickly as possible for two reasons: a flapping spinnaker creates enormous drag on the reach (as opposed to the run where this drag is actually in the right direction), and it is very likely to get twisted during a slow hoist.

The kite is best launched from the leeward side in the lee of mainsail and jib, which means that you need to take this into account when preparing it before the start or when taking it

Above: A spinnaker hoist from the leeward bag.

down. Generally this means stowing it on the port side if the weather mark is to port or the starboard side if the first mark is to starboard. The photo sequences show how to launch the kite both from the windward and the leeward side. Note that you always pull the kite down on the windward side.

Below: If the kite is in the windward bag you will need to do a chuck hoist.

The spinnaker chute

If your boat has a spinnaker chute then many of these problems are solved.

Advantages   So long as the chute is of large diameter the spinnaker will go up quite fast. The helmsman can pull it up while the crew sheets it in, so it will rarely get twisted. It is also very easily doused: as the crew attends to the spinnaker pole the helmsman simply releases the continuous halyard and pulls rapidly on the downhaul line. However, if the halyard is allowed to run before the downhaul is pulled in the spinnaker can end up under the bow of the boat which spells real disaster!

Disadvantages   The spinnaker chute itself adds weight to the front of the boat, and even more weight if water is trapped inside the spinnaker. A flap over the mouth of the chute will deflect water to some degree.

Below: Good crew work – keep the guy and sheet in your hands, pull the guy back as far as possible, then let out the sheet until the spinnaker luff curls. Repeat constantly.

Left: Pull the guy back on the run to present more sail area to the wind. If the pole is too far forward (far left) the spinnaker is blanketed by the main.

spinnaker reaches with their poles too low. This makes the spinnaker too full at the front. Raising the pole flattens the leading edge, allowing better pointing for a given setting. Overtrimming the sheet will badly backwind the mainsail. Keep easing the sheet until the luff is on the point of falling in.

Close reaching

A good reaching spinnaker can be used effectively even if the apparent wind is ahead of abeam. Skill and experience helps greatly on this point of sailing.

The pole needs to be well forward but, if possible, not quite against the jib luff. The guy needs to be cleated close to the weather shroud since even a small degree of stretch affects the pole angle greatly. In order to sheet the spinnaker sufficiently to keep it pulling, some backwinding of the mainsail is inevitable. To minimise this, ease the kicking strap (vang) and trim the mainsheet towards the centreline. Raising the boom in this way also reduces its chances of hitting the water should you heel excessively, frees the spinnaker sheet (which raises the clew of the kite slightly), and reduces the heeling moment of the mainsail by opening the top of the sail. You will need to hike harder to offset the extra side forces. Raise your board

Running

When running the pole should be pulled right aft to expose the maximum area of the sail to the wind. The tack and clew (the two bottom corners) should be set at approximately the same height by adjusting the pole height. The sheet is then eased until the weather edge (the luff) is just about to collapse.

Reaching

As the apparent wind moves forward let the pole go forward and pull in the sheet. At this point it may pay to raise the pole a few inches.

Many inexperienced crews sail slowly on

Right: Adjust the pole so that the tack and clew are level. This makes the sail symmetrical, and it will curl more evenly at the luff. The pole is too high on the left, too low on the right.

to about halfway to help reduce heeling.

There are two good reasons why you may decide *not* to carry your spinnaker on the close reach:

1 Because the reach is just too close to the wind for it to pay off. That is, the extra forward drive may be so slight that the very act of putting up and taking down the sail will lose you more than you will gain. In general, if the halyard points abeam or aft of abeam, the spinnaker is not paying and should be taken down.

2 Because the wind is too strong, and the böat will heel too much, spilling wind and making it difficult to hold a course above or on the line to the next mark.

In the first case you must rely on experience or watch the other boats to determine the best course of action. In the second case, again watch the rest of the fleet. As a beginner the best advice is: if in doubt don't use your spinnaker on a close reach if it's windy. However, as you gain experience a good rule of thumb is: if you are not sitting out hard *without* it up (or, on a trapeze boat, the crew is not on the wire) then you will

probably be able to hold the spinnaker with the increased leverage available.

Gybing the spinnaker

The spinnaker adds a little more interest to gybing. When you are proficient you should be able to complete the gybe without the spinnaker collapsing, but this takes practice!

The procedure is this. Pull the leeward twinning line in tight and release the weather one. Bear away, rolling the boat to weather. Just before the boom comes over the crew should pull the pole back so that the spinnaker swings round and sets on the new leeward side. He should then remove the pole end from the mast

Below: Gybing the spinnaker. Once the boom has gone across the helmsman steers with his legs while holding the sheet and guy, to keep the kite full throughout the manoeuvre.

Golden rules

★ Always put up the kite before the start to check it.

★ Only fly a spinnaker if the halyard is pointing forward of abeam (and if you can keep the boat upright).

★ Try to stow the spinnaker so it is launched from the leeward side.

★ Always take the spinnaker down to windward.

★ Always ease the sheet as much as possible.

★ Adjust the pole height so the tack and clew of the spinnaker are equal heights above the water.

★ Raise the pole on a close reach.

Above: On a reach, ease the sheet to keep the spinnaker leech away from the main (right).

and clip it to the new guy before disconnecting the other end (from the new sheet) and attaching it to the mast. After the gybe the helmsman can hold the sheet and guy while standing astride the tiller. In this way the boat can be steered straight and the spinnaker kept full. Finally the crew takes over the sheet and guy, and the boat is away on the new gybe.

Practice is essential, particularly when gybing from a reach to a reach which is more difficult, for the helmsman is not able to hold the sheets. Always remember to gybe the boat when *you* want to, and don't let the boat decide the moment for you.

Below: To lower the spinnaker, take off the pole and stow it, then pull the sail down into the windward bag while the helmsman progressively releases the halyard.

Glossary

Bearing away   Altering course away from the wind.
Blanketing   Positioning yourself between your opponent and the wind, to reduce the wind available to him.
Camber   The curve or belly in a sail.
Committee boat   The boat which controls the race, usually moored at one end of the start line.
Covering   Staying between your opponent and the next mark.
Dirty wind   The turbulent wind to leeward of a sail and in line with it.
Feathering   A temporary and subtle luff, on a beat, to depower the sails.
Foils   The rudder blade and centreboard.
Free (also called Footing)   Sailing a little off the wind on a beat, with sheets eased, to improve speed at the expense of pointing ability.
Gate start   A method of starting a one-design fleet where a port tack boat beats across the fleet, the other boats passing under her stern.
Handicap race   A method of racing boats of different classes together, using a handicap to correct for their different speeds.
Header   A windshift, so the wind comes more from the bow.
In irons   Stopped head to wind, unintentionally.
Inner distance mark (IDM)   A buoy laid approximately on the startline near the committee boat. Competitors may not pass between the two.
Layline   Imaginary lines depicting the port and starboard close-hauled courses to the windward mark.
Lee-bow effect   When one boat, slightly ahead and to leeward, deflects wind onto the lee side of a pursuing boat's sails.
Lee helm   A boat which bears away if the tiller is released when beating has lee helm.
Leeward boat   A boat downwind of another.
Leeward mark   The mark rounded at the beginning of the beat. The most downwind mark of the course (except for starting marks).
Luff   Altering course towards the wind.
Mast rake   How far aft the mast leans.
Olympic course   A course arranged around three buoys giving beat, reach, reach, beat, run, beat.
Officer of the day (OOD)   The person in charge of racing on a particular day.
Overlap   An overlap exists when the bow of a pursuing boat is ahead of an imaginary line through the aftmost point of the leading boat, and at right angles to that boat.

Pinch   Beat too close to the wind.
Pointing   A boat sailing very close to the wind is said to be pointing well, although she may be a little slower in the water than a boat sailing free.
Protest   A protest is lodged by flying a red protest flag. The protest meeting is similar to a court of law.
Pursuit race   Boats start at times determined by their handicap, and the first across the line is the winner.
Rhumb line   The direct line to the next mark.
Roll tack   A light weather tack in which the boat is rolled, thus fanning the sails through the air.
Safe leeward position   The leading yacht establishes herself in front and to leeward of her opponent (see lee-bow effect).
Sailing instructions   Written instructions on the management of a race, and the course to be sailed.
720   If the sailing instructions allow it, doing two complete circles can exonerate a boat after certain infringements.
Starboard!   If two yachts are on opposite tacks (have different windward sides) the one on starboard tack has right of way.
Tacking downwind   Sailing downwind in a series of broad reaches, connected by gybes, to try and reach the leeward mark faster.
Transit   Two fixed objects aligned to give an imaginary line or bearing.
Up, up, up!   The leeward boat is requesting the windward boat to luff.
Water!   A request for room to round a mark or obstruction, or to tack clear of an object.
Weather helm   A boat which luffs when the tiller is let go has weather helm.
Weather mark   The most windward mark of the course, excepting finishing marks.
Wetted area   The surface of the hull that is immersed.
Wind backs   When the wind shifts anticlockwise.
Windbend   A progressive windshift, i.e. one that becomes more pronounced as you travel into it.
Windshadow   The area to leeward of a sail where the wind is lessened.
Windshift   A change in the direction of the wind.
Wind veers   When the wind shifts clockwise.
Windward boat   The boat that is nearer the wind.

RACE SIGNALS

The meanings of visual and sound signals are stated below. An arrow pointing up or down (▲ ▼) means that a visual signal is displayed or removed. A dot (•) means a sound; dots with dashes (• - - - •) mean repetitive sounds. When a visual signal is displayed over a class flag, the signal applies only to that class.

COLOUR CODE
Blue   Red   Yellow

Postponement Signals

AP Races not started are *postponed*. The warning signal will be made 1 minute after removal unless at that time the race is *postponed* again or *abandoned*.
▲ • • ▼ •

AP over H Races not started are *postponed*. Further signals ashore.
▲ • •

AP over A Races not started are *postponed*. No more racing today.
▲ • •

Penant 1 ▲ • • ▼ •

Penant 2 ▲ • • ▼ •

Penant 3 ▲ • • ▼ •

Penant 4 ▲ • • ▼ •

Penant 5 ▲ • • ▼ •

Penant 6 ▲ • • ▼ •

A-P over a numeral pennant 1-6 *Postponement* of 1-6 hours from the scheduled startig time

Abandonment Signals

N All races that have started are *abandoned*. Return to the starting area. The warning signal will be made 1 minute after removal unless at that time the race is *abandoned* again or *postponed*.
▲ • • • ▼ •

N over H All races are *abandoned*. Further signals ashore.
▲ • • •

N over A All races are *abandoned*. No more racing today.
▲ • • •

Recall Signals

X Individual recall.
▲ •

First Substitute General recall. The warning signal will be made 1 minute after removal.
• - - - •

Signals before the Start

P Preparatory signal.
▲ • ▼ •

I Rule 30.1 is in effect.
▲ • ▼ •

Z Rule 30.2 is in effect.
▲ • ▼ •

Black flag. Rule 30.3 is in effect.
▲ • ▼ •

Course Change

S No later than the warning signal: Sail the short course. At a rounding or finishing *mark*: *Finish* between the nearby *mark* and the staff displaying this flag.
▲ • •

C The position of the next *mark* has been changed.
• - - - •

Other Signals

L Ashore: A notice to competitors has been posted. Afloat: Come within hail or follow this boat.
▲ •

M The object displaying this signal replaces a missing *mark*.
• - - - •

Y Wear personal buoyancy.
▲ •

(no sound)
Blue flag or shape. This race committee boat is in position at the finishing line.